Open Boat Cruising

Open Boat Cruising

John Glasspool

illustrated by Peter A. G. Milne

First published in Great Britain by
NAUTICAL PUBLISHING CO LTD
Lymington, Hampshire, S04 9BA

ISBN 0 245 51874 6

Filmset and printed in Great Britain by
BAS Printers Limited, Wallop, Hampshire

CONTENTS

LIST OF ILLUSTRATIONS

Introduction

The best way to learn the basic arts of sailing is by going out for a few hours each day in a centreboard dinghy. This is indeed how most people have learned, but later they progress to variations such as dinghy racing, family cruising in a cabin yacht, long distance cruising, perhaps as a crew, or passage and offshore racing.

Less heard of, but well established, is genuine dinghy cruising where several days or perhaps much longer, are spent sailing as independently as larger cruising vessels. Those who sail in this way are scattered around the coast and as individualists are less likely, than say members of dinghy racing clubs, to exchange ideas frequently and thus benefit from mutual experience. This book has therefore been written to increase confidence in open boat cruising as well as give ideas and suggestions—rather than exact instruction— on how to go about it.

It is assumed that the rudiments of sailing are known to the reader together with the ordinary definitions and terms used in small boats. Because of the nature of dinghy cruising, it gets a minimum of coverage in the yachting press compared with racing events or long voyages. A few outstanding voyages in open boats have become widely known and can give tremendous interest and reassurance to sailors of the same types of dinghy. But it would not be right for the majority to attempt to emulate them: they are mentioned later in this book in the context of a type of open boat cruising suitable for everyone.

1 Why dinghies?

Dinghies are at the lower end of the sailing yacht scale in terms of size, but at the other when it comes to popularity. It is because a really small boat can be brought ashore, kept at home and maintained without much effort that it is of such wide appeal. For a dinghy used for cruising these advantages multiply for she can be simply rigged, avoiding expensive equipment. She can become, too, within a few seconds a rowing boat or an outboard motor boat which has shallow enough draft to explore creeks and beaches, frequented or remote.

Too often we tend to forget that, with livings to earn, our boats spend most of their time idle. Twenty years ago it was true that boats, unlike horses, didn't eat anything. Today the fact has to be faced that after the basic cost of the keel boat the biggest item by far in her annual budget is to pay for somewhere for her to lie afloat doing nothing. A dinghy needs water only for sailing. For the rest of the time she can be left on a trolley in a dinghy pound or on a road trailer in a back garden.

To a plain boat, gear can be added as it can be afforded: without frills, she costs little to keep, while offering as much fun to the individual as a larger craft. The sense of achievement in crossing stretches of water five or ten miles wide, is hardly less than that of a yacht crew which does a hundred mile passage in the open sea.

I do not claim that a dinghy cruise is more fun than a chance to go foreign; merely that for the sort of sailing most people do— two days a week at most, sometimes three—there is a lot to be said for doing it in the simplest, cheapest way possible, which is in a small centreboard boat, light enough to be handled ashore by the people who would normally sail in her, and seaworthy enough, with prudent sailing, to offer miles of coastwise cruising or the more intimate exploration of creeks and estuaries.

For men and women of average fitness and fortitude, dinghy cruising can offer all the challenges of seamanship, coastal navigation, and tide and weather knowledge that a larger boat can. Scope for preparing and serving sustaining food is only a little less on a dinghy camping cruise than in the three-sided tea chest which goes by the name of galley on many a so-called family cruiser.

**A Good
Seaboat**
A cruising dinghy must be a seaboat first and a carrier second although she must be expected to carry far more gear than even a conservatively-shaped racing dinghy. Too often, family cruisers are designed from the inside and the hull wrapped around the accommodation, with the effect on their sailing performance well known to every dinghy sailor who has beaten them hands down to windward.

This is not intended as a knock at the opposition, just as an illustration that because a boat is decked to keep the home comforts dry she is not necessarily a better boat than one which is not.

Physical requirements of dinghy cruising need only be modest. One does not need to be a super person to make a day long passage in an open boat—you might if you fail to study the weather, of course—but I reckon that the secret ingredient which makes a dinghy cruiser is more mind than muscle.

Nobody who sails on the sea escapes a dusting for ever. In a dinghy, even a moderate sea breeze piping up suddenly on a warm day can seem daunting at first, until the crew have time to know its boat and have confidence in her. From this confidence, which comes from sailing as often as possible, stems the nerve the open-boat man needs to stay the boss when the breeze begins to freshen and the first of the weather-going tide begins to show its fangs against the breeze. As for the physical hardships, good clothing and intelligently planned cooking and sleeping arrangements can ensure these are by no means great.

Lightness
A proper cruising dinghy tries to combine the lightness and sea-grace of a curragh or a kayak with the habitability of a small yacht. Many people have, in different ways, achieved a working compromise between these two extremes.

The important thing to remember is that open boat cruising can be whatever you want to make it. The dinghy is the most versatile of boats. Frank Dye and Peter Clutterbuck have made voyages which would be a credit to quite large yachts. But anybody who settles for something more modest—a passage down the coast to a pleasant estuary, say, or a holiday exploring the Solent, the East coast rivers or (with more experience) the Western Isles—can be sure his sense of achievement will be just as great, and his haul of adventure just as rich for being on a smaller scale.

The open boat cruiser can best appreciate Hilaire Belloc's observation that 'he who goes to sea in a little boat learns terror and salvation, happy living, air, danger, exultation, glory and repose at the end' if he does no more than sail to some new place for a week-end, cooking, sleeping and exploring and sailing home on Sunday.

Single-handed
From the deck of a larger yacht a dinghy might seem a frail and vulnerable thing. But good boats are not judged by size alone.

Fig. 1 'probing in towards a strange deserted land'

A dinghy bound a'cruising, with gear that enables her to reef snugly
in a breeze, and with nothing flimsy about her, can give the crew
a pride in her gameness often missing aboard a bigger vessel where
in average weather, sailing is just a matter of pointing her in the
required direction and trimming the sails accordingly.

This sense of companionship with the boat, which wise old
Belloc could have added to his list, occurred to me strongly at
dawn one day, sailing alone, when the shore was lost in a haze, and
she stood off close-hauled to where the seas of the main tide were
running against the breeze.

All around was racket and noise. The white crests grated like
shingle as they curled over and fell down the slate faces. They
slapped and fretted against the weather side and volleyed the jib
and bottom boards with grapeshots of spray. The grey sea seemed to
speed past only four inches below the lee gunwale, but she was
reefed enough and she heeled no more. The warm mahogany
gleamed comfortingly against the grey waste (distrust any man who
says he 'loves the sea'; he's never seen it) and the rough tiller and
sodden mainsheet tugged like living things.

It was late October, and the loneliness of winter was in the air.
In the circle of sea curtained off all about the boat by the slow
clearing night fog, there was no other craft not even a bird. I put her
about and stood in towards the hidden shore again to catch sight of
Gilkicker, squat and lifeless like a ghostly Elsinore, come through
darkly on the port bow.

Here we were, this boat and I, in one of the busiest places
around the coast, yet we could have been probing in towards a
strange deserted land. (Fig. 1.) The cold air groped into my neck
where the damp scarf had worked loose. I stuffed it back into place,
and gave up staring around at this bleak hostility and concentrated
on getting the boat along. Now and then a sea would swing her up,
setting the jib quivering. As she bore off again the crunch of the
wavetops against the clinker planks resumed their rhythm.

Seaworthy   It had been a night sail to catch the tide for Portsmouth, and
though Small   after a sleepless night such a morning can seem menacing and
awful. Dawn in a small boat usually is. But the boat was capable
and busy. She restored the balance and with a recovered sense of
proportion came appetite for breakfast. I took the mainsheet in
the tiller hand and reached in the stern locker for a flask of tea
made the previous night before this eerie marathon began. The tea
was black and stale, but blessedly hot and reviving. There were
clammy sandwiches to eat with it, and afterwards things seemed
altogether brighter as the daylight strengthened and the mist began
to clear. There were small fishing boats anchored on the edge of
the shoals off Stokes Bay, and a car ferry glided by on the edge of
visibility. We were back in the living world again.

I had expected a dusting as we tacked out again into the tide
to clear Gilkicker but the seas though steeper, had no malice in

Fig. 2   Even dinghies must carry riding lights in order to anchor
safely

them. At last the sheets could be eased and she whooped away on
a broad reach down the sea wall towards Portsmouth Harbour. Pride
in one's boat, in such a small boat, is immense after a sail like that.
But I admit it increases with thinking about it afterwards in comfort.

In contrast, there was a summer night, with a full moon and the
smell of trees and grass off the land, as we ghosted towards Cowes
on the last of the breeze, watching the sky darken to westward
and catching the faint sound of voices over the water from the yachts
gathered for the Round the Island Race next day.

We took a rough transit of the Royal Yacht Squadron flagstaff over
the end of the Shrape breakwater, nosed into the shallow water and
anchored in three feet. It was just after low water and we could lie
for the night there, safe as houses out of the traffic, yet with a
clear view to run in for shelter if the breeze piped up from eastward
during the night. When the breeze finally died we lay at anchor in

a perfect mirror. To seaward there was a murmur of engines as Round the Island latecomers made their way in. The town was packed with the crews so we put off the jostle at the pontoons for a late night look at the town, and stayed put to enjoy the tranquil evening.

There was no fear of large traffic where we lay, but several small fishing boats were skirting the edge of the Shrape mud in and out of harbour, so I rigged a small battery lantern on the forestay as a riding light. (Fig. 2.) We partially unrolled the tent cover over the boom to keep the dew out of the boat, but left the after part open to sit and smoke and watch the sights in as much comfort as in the cockpit of a four-tonner. The noises ashore gradually ceased; we unrolled sleeping bags, set the alarm clock and slept, watched the vast race fleet get under way at dawn, then went ashore for a hotel breakfast before continuing our planned cruise to Poole.

These are the sort of modest cruising adventures which are in mind throughout this book, easily within reach of anybody competent to sail a boat, and who wants a change from the normal Sunday afternoon dinghy sail. Graduate to longer, more ambitious voyages when you will, that feeling of independence from the shore which is one of the chief delights of any sort of cruising can be captured even in the crowded ways of rivers and estuaries.

2 First ventures

The point has to be made firmly that dinghy cruising is not for novices. The would-be cruiser first has to learn to sail, then to walk before he runs by making short expeditions in safe waters before tackling ambitious sailing on open water far away from help and moral support.

Cruising in open boats can be uncomfortable. But then, so can sailing an ocean racer across the Channel in a force six and driving rain, and so can the pounding of a power boat bucking a steep sea on the way west to Torquay. The best planned cruises in the early days are those which allow for shelter within easy reach if the weather turns sour, and with a safe anchorage and camping site at the end of a reasonable day's sail.

There will be occasions when, to use a favourable tide or to take advantage of a steady breeze, or merely because it is a lovely night, passages will be made after dark. Night sailing is a skill which should be practised thoroughly in the familiar surroundings of one's home waters, and needs experience in reading and interpreting navigation lights of other craft, and being able to plot one's way by the lights of buoys and beacons. Good torches are a vital part of the cruising dinghy's equipment. Several of them. And if a cruise is to last several days, they should have spare batteries and bulbs as well. The rubber-cased torches which are available from most hardware stores are all right, although they cannot be relied upon to be completely watertight. When sailing at night a powerful torch should be kept within easy reach of the helmsman at all times.

Navigation lights

If it is possible to fit navigation lights they are probably worth the trouble. But, in a dinghy they are almost sure to be too low or too small to be visible to other traffic. The international regulations for prevention of collision at sea allow a small boat, or a rowing boat under sail to shine a white light when it wants to reveal its presence to another vessel. But at night, even more than during the daytime, it is folly to stand on course if it is clear that a larger vessel would have to alter to avoid a smaller one. Never mind the

rights and wrongs, if you are the smaller boat, be prepared to keep
out of everybody's way.

Everybody who goes in a boat on navigable waters has the
responsibility for learning what flags, light and sound signals mean.
There is no excuse for the dinghy sailor to think that because his is
small fry, these things have no relevance for him.

He should know enough of the language of the sea to be able to
steer an intelligent course, without the timid and erratic behaviour
which causes confusion to other craft nearby. Racing people often
affect a superior ignorance of these things, which does nothing to
endear them to working boat skippers, divers or rescue services.
A dinghy cruiser should consider himself a more proficient seaman
in this respect, especially when he plans to visit waters and harbours
which are new to him.

**Night
Sailing**

When sailing at night, when the breeze is anywhere free, it is
a good plan after dark to stow the jib. This vastly increases the
helmsman's range of vision and makes one distraction less from what
is going on around him. It is important to avoid shining torches or
bright lights close to one's eyes. For this can impare night vision
for several vital minutes. On open waters a crew might be able to
take watchkeeping in a more relaxed way. Close inshore, with other
yachts, ferries, fishing craft, coasters, and tankers to-ing and
fro-ing, the crew cannot afford to relax vigilance too long.

But take heart. It is not as desperate as it sounds. In good
weather the field of vision is vast and ships move across it at
comparatively slow speed. There is always plenty of time to steer a
safe course if you maintain a running picture of what is going on.
Remember also that, compared with larger craft, dinghies are nimble
creatures which can turn quickly away from a dicey-looking
situation. This is an advantage which often makes up for their lack
of speed.

**Keeping
Alert**

An important rule for passage making, by night or day, is to
eat and drink frequently. A couple of biscuits and a hot drink from
a flask will do wonders for one's alertness and confidence. Chocolate
and boiled sweets are useful snacks also. Eating under way calls
for food which is eaten one-handed. Sandwiches, cold sausages
and the like. Delicate creations which threaten to collapse over the
bottom boards if roughly handled are to be avoided. Save the more
elaborate meals until sailing is over for the day, but nibble often
when on passage.

One of the advantages of fitting out for a dinghy cruise is that
you have far less to cart aboard than the owner of a yacht, simply
because there is not room for it. Built-in lockers might seem a
good idea in a cruising dinghy, with lots of space around the sides
to stow things out of the wet. Unfortunately it never seems to
work out that way. Any locker in an open boat, no matter how well
made, gets damp after only a little time. Rusty shackles, old mackerel
spinners and siezed-up pliers tend to get pushed into them and

forgotten when the cruise is over. Match heads turn to soggy paste and unused batteries bleed their corrosive substance to the detriment of gear stowed away in the future.

Stowage

For cruising, it is a good plan to have a waterproof container, whether specially-made plywood boxes or large containers of the Tupperware type, each of which is allocated its own place in the boat, where it can be lashed or secured with shock cord. This method pays off when the time comes to beach the boat and the whole lot can be removed within minutes to help lighten ship. It is handy too, for crews who camp ashore to carry a couple of large containers rather than an armful of odds and ends dug out of lockers. However, for small oddments which should be kept with the boat at all times, such as bosun's gear, there is a lot to be said for a small locker under the stern thwart. This is easy enough to make, on the same principle as the dry stowage locker mentioned elsewhere. (Fig. 3.)

If the thwart can be removed, as it ought to, then the locker is made so that it can be screw-fastened up into the thwart. When measuring up for the job, be extra careful to see that the dimensions of the proposed locker will clear the turn of the bilge, the bottom boards and the projecting stern knee behind it. An easier alternative to a locker with a door is a drawer, fitted to slide on a pair of runners screwed into the thwart, with a turnbuckle stop to prevent it sliding out by accident, and with a strip of canvas weighted with a batten, tacked to the thwart and positioned to hang down over the top of the drawer and thus prevent spray getting in.

Buoyancy

A lot of space has to be sacrificed in a dinghy to buoyancy, which is even more important when she is sailing on her own and away from the attendant safety craft which accompany races. Some lockers are made with watertight hatches, sealed with foam rubber washers, which are supposed to act as buoyancy as well as dry stowage—an unreasonable assumption when the locker is crammed tight with tinned food, warps and tools.

I think the most reliable form of buoyancy is still the airbag, the bright red or yellow p.v.c. sausage which can be firmly attached under thwarts or benches with webbing straps. Reliable not because of its toughness—although in years of cruising I have never yet punctured one—but because it contains the most effective buoyancy material ever devised—air.

One glance or a prod from a finger can show if it is in working order, and it can be removed easily when the boat is laid up or needs painting. Bags can well be protected against chafe and pinching if they are fitted with jackets, easily made of waterproof flax canvas or heavyweight Torylene.

When sleeping aboard, an airbag makes a more comfortable shoulder rest than a rigid locker, and if room for sleeping is very restricted it can be deflated, provided it is blown up again before the cruise resumes. As for sealed, built-in buoyancy tanks, which are common in glass fibre boats, it seems a bad idea to have such large

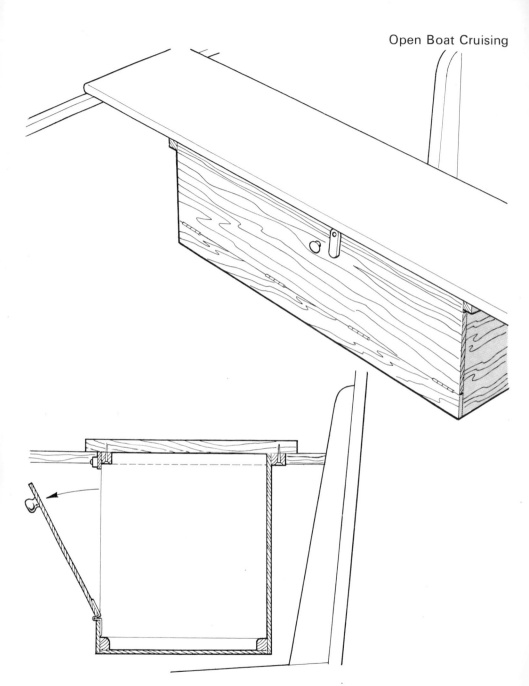

Fig. 3 A suitable locker under the stern thwart in a wooden dinghy. The locker is completely removable and merely screwed up under the thwart for cruising.

areas of the hull cut off from inspection and maintenance in this way.

Glass fibre, we all know, requires little maintenance, yet I have known more than one case where the joint between the hull and the buoyancy tank fractured and was only discovered when water was heard sloshing about inside when the boat was hoisted on to its trolley. Getting that water out was another story altogether.

The simplest way to test dinghy cruising as a sport is to try it in its simplest form, namely a week-end with one or perhaps two nights away. If the reality proves as much fun as the fancy, then one can learn enough from early short cruises of this kind to whet the appetite for longer ventures during holidays. Certainly it only takes a week-end jaunt in our climate to test the soundness and suitability of boat, gear, camping equipment and clothing, and one returns from these trial voyages with mind full of ideas for improving, replacing, or dispensing with altogether. If the boat is trailed to the sea by car, the first lesson one learns is the difference in weight between a racing boat and one crammed with cruising gear, so make sure the car and the trailer can cope with the weight.

Making Plans
Dinghies are more vulnerable to weather changes than yachts, but all the same it is useful to have a planned route for the cruise whenever possible. Relatives will, of course, be grateful to be let in on this, but the main virtue of a plan is to succeed in sticking to it. Realistic plans, and later ones made in the light of experience, will be based on a modest mileage only. In dinghies, the mere distance travelled is not important. A feature of a seamanlike cruise plan is to take into account not only the chosen route, but all the other places within reach if weather or inclination decides a change of plan.

It must be remembered that waters famed for their scenery and freedom from buildings can be the loneliest for a boat in need of help. Places like the west country and the Scottish islands are as beautiful seascapes as any, but the beauty counts for nothing when a fast tide turns ugly against a freshening breeze. On the other hand somewhere like Southampton Water, has more dreary scenery but less startling also is the effect of the wind and sea.

The crew which chooses solitude must be equipped for it. This means careful compiling and checking of lists before sailing to make sure that taken-for-granted things like matches, saucepan, bottle opener, fresh water and other necessaries, are included. Part of the fun of cruising is to go ashore and shop. But sailing boats have a perverse habit of delaying their arrival anywhere until the shops are shut, so it pays always to have at least one square meal in the making aboard; bacon and sausage, for example, tinned beans, and other delicacies beloved of cruising men.

The boat herself should be remembered in the planning and packing. Every boat should have her bosun's bag, come-in-handy bag, call it what you will, which contains spare shackles, coils of thin line and twine, a spare plug for the outboard, sewing needles, packed in a greased tin, for sail and tent repairs, and other bits and pieces.

For longer cruises in really lonely waters, simple woodworking tools and a resin repair kit if the hull is g.r.p. are also necessary. These items make the boat more independent of the shore, and are an insurance against the boat's efficiency being imperilled by minor breakages or gear failures which the crew can remedy themselves.

A log is well worth keeping (more about this in a later chapter) and also aboard should be a large scale chart of the cruise waters, a map of the coastal land and a tide table. An invaluable companion, especially in a dinghy where there is neither time nor room for pencil and paper work, is a tide atlas which tells at a glance the strength and set of the main currents around the coast for each hour.

Also worth the space it takes up is a radio. Just a small transistor, with a sound polythene bag to wrap it in. The radio's main job in a boat is to provide weather forecasts, but it can be good company as well. Crews of other boats within earshot in a tranquil anchorage may not think so, however, so bear in mind how well sound travels across water and keep the volume turned down.

Dinghy Cruising Association

One or two weekend cruises will be enough to show if open-boat cruising is for you or not. If it is, and the idea of meeting similar minded people appeals, it will be a good idea to join the Dinghy Cruising Association. This was formed in 1955 to encourage cruising under sail in dinghies and in small cabin boats which have some of the handling characteristics of dinghies. (See Appendix)

Greatest benefit of membership is the Association's quarterly Bulletin, which is mailed to members. This contains cruising yarns descriptions of members' boats, advice on converting boats for cruising and pilot guides to likely cruising waters. In addition, the Association organizes lectures, film shows, and week-end rallies around the coast. The Secretary is Ernest Baily, 12, Spencers Road, Maidenhead, Berks.

Cruising folk are individualistic, and none more so, it seems, than those who cruise in dinghies. So the Association does not try to impose any organization in the way a racing club has to do. Its strength lies in boat owners throughout the country who might never turn up at meetings but who, in an occasional line in the Bulletin about a cruise or their boat, makes the Association the most ready and important source of practical knowledge.

The fascination of dinghy cruising lies in the fact that getting started costs so little—boats suitable for cruising are about the cheapest going, particularly second hand ones. No expensive gear will make an owner a better boatman than he will be with one basic requirement—a good, simple boat.

3 Types

The more a man gets used to a particular type of boat and becomes confident in her ways, the more versatile he can make her. Uffa Fox used to go single-handed cruising in a sailing canoe—and used to take his best suit so that he could call on friends when he went ashore; Patrick Ellam, in the book 'Sopranino' described how a sailing canoe was his trial horse in his quest for a seaboat as small and light as possible, and described some lively Channel crossings in one.

Coble men of the North East coast of England aver that theirs are the only open boats for serious open water work. The same applies to the galley enthusiasts of Cornwall and the Isles of Scilly, the Curragh men of western Ireland and the Eskimo kayak men of Greenland as well. The boat type one is most familiar with is the best bet for a trial dinghy cruiser, but there are limitations. A Fireball dinghy is one of the most exhilarating boats ever designed, but the only cruising gear she could carry is that which the crew could cram into oilskin pockets. Any dinghy can be used for day sailing, and only a few would be too demanding for a week-end amble with a wife and kids aboard. Rather fewer boats adapt easily to cruising and there are still fewer boats which are fun to race and which at the same time have stowage space and reasonable comfort for a crew who plan an extended sail with several nights away.

In racing, all the crew's mind and muscle is given to getting the boat along. In cruising, as in the old working boats, the occupants are often more interested in what is happening outside the boat, when exploring a new stretch of coast or piloting their way into a strange estuary for example.

They need a boat docile enough to behave herself when their attention wanders to checking landmarks against the chart, or when they are being captivated by the scenery of a wooded bay they are sailing into for the first time. How boring it would be to come across such a place at the end of a day's sail in a highly bred boat which frets if the crew's attention wanders for a second. Choose a slow coach boat for cruising, I suggest. After all, any small open boat is the slowest and most uncertain means of transport there is. A bicycle is like a train compared with it.

There will be adventures enough afloat without having to travel fast to find them, and a comfortable passage can do more for the morale of the crew than an impressively fast time from launching point to destination. You can go fast in a well defined triangle of water off the home club. Cruising is a more reflective pastime.

An important requirement of a cruising dinghy is that she should be capable of being sailed single-handed, even when there is company aboard. On a cruise, the crewman has lots of better things to do than sit all day holding a jibsheet. Things like serving sandwiches, pouring hot drinks from flasks, flaking the anchor warp down ready for use, spotting harbour entrances against a jumbled background of buildings or cliffs, or tuning into the radio weather forecast, or merely taking it easy.

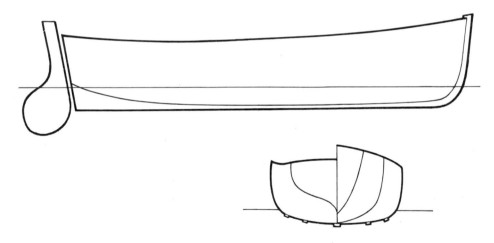

Fig. 4   Profile and section of a dinghy suitable for cruising. Note hard bilge, flat bottom and ample freeboard. Rudder is moderate in depth and extreme racing shapes are not present.

Too Large a Boat

It is a mistake to choose a dinghy which is too big and heavy to handle *ashore and afloat* by the number of crew which are available to sail in her. There is a notion that the bigger the boat the more safe she will be. So she might, provided there are muscular shipmates enough to launch her and to sail her. But a big dinghy, sailed single-handed, is a tiring, frightening and often dangerous creature. Two men might be cramped in a twelve footer, but they will be able to handle her without effort and haul her up a slipway or smooth beach unaided. This knowledge, that there are enough hands

to cope with the size of the boat and to keep her romping along at
her best in a breeze, is good for morale.

If by temperament, or through lack of a regular crew who can
be counted on to turn up when a cruise is planned, the owner prefers
to go single-handed, I would suggest he think hard before committing
himself to anything larger than twelve feet overall. There are
hundreds of fine open centreboarders larger than this, with the
sailplan adapted or reduced which are regularly sailed solo. But
beaching them is a problem nigh impossible, and if a dinghy is too
heavy to beach, then why not go the whole hog and settle for a
decked yacht?

**A Cruising
Comeback**

At the last two or three boat shows at Earls Court there has
been a slight increase in the number of dinghies and open dayboats
designed for cruising or pottering as a change from racing. So a
man who wants a boat for the job is now less dependent on the
surviving veterans which boat yards around the coast used to produce
as stock jobs, or the outclassed, heavy 'Middling-on-the-mud,
one-design' classes which used to be the backbone of small club
racing fleets until the home-building boom soon after the war.

The man who wants 'a real boat', meaning one of sturdy
traditional model and suggesting good seaworthy characteristics,
is now more likely to find what he is looking for new, rather than
in the small ads. of local newspapers. And gentle irony, we have
had to wait for glass fibre construction to become almost universal
for this hark-back to come about. (Fig. 4.)

I like wood. For no more rational reason than that I like the look
and feel of it, and favour the opportunity to shift the positions of
cleats, fairleads or other fittings according to choice, and because
wood stands up to harsh treatment better than the vulnerable gel
coat of g.r.p. Just as a gardener accepts the work to enjoy the
flowers, so I accept the frequent attention with sandpaper and
varnish as worthwhile to keep a wooden boat looking her best.
With wood, especially if it is finished in clear varnish, the condition
of the timber is always open to inspection. Builders who specialize
in wooden boats are becoming rare. But one thing the boat hunter
soon learns is that there are many more boat-builders at work
around the coast than ever get a mention at boat shows.

**Builders in
Wood**

Within the area where I live there are active builders at Portsmouth,
Hill Head and Bembridge, Isle of Wight, still turning out wooden
boats in the traditional way. So if you want a new boat built of
wood, it pays to take a trip to the seaside and the waterside districts
of long established harbours. These old craftsmen are sometimes
too reticent in advertising their trade, but they can be found.

One who still regularly exhibits at the boat show each year is
Mr. L. H. Walker, of Leigh on Sea, Essex, whose twelve foot Tideway
Class dinghies, fourteen-footers and Yachting World Dayboats, all in
mahogany clinker, hold their own against the g.r.p. competition

all around.
   If you have a wooden boat, be prepared to look after it.
The fashion today is to expect to trolley a boat into a corner of a
dinghy pound and forget it until next time, or even to forget it for
the whole of the winter. Wooden boats are more demanding, but in
return they set up an owner like a Savile Row suit in a world of
off-the-peg glass fibre.
   If you believe, and probably rightly, that boats are there to be

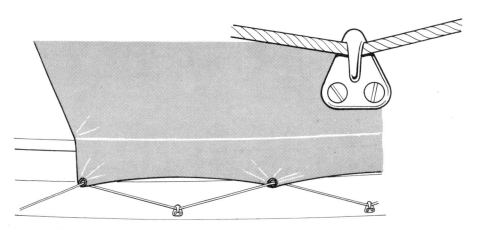

Fig. 5   Lacing hooks are invariably required for rigging tents or
awnings

used, and that tinkering with them ashore is a waste of sailing
time, or if commitments simply rule out days for a mid-season coat
of varnish or paint, then you will choose g.r.p.
   The material, which has been with us long enough now to be
called 'traditional' glass fibre to distinguish it from expanded
plastics, mouldings and other developments, has had at least two
blessed effects on dinghy design. Hull shapes have broken free of
the slab-sided look which plywood construction made common, and
deterioration by the elements is virtually impossible.

Faults of   My only regret is that when the designer or builder decrees that
GRP   a jib sheet lead or toestrap attachment or buoyancy tank shall be
                  fixed at such a place, there they have to stay. Handy attachment
                  points are always in demand in a small sailing boat, and in too many
                  g.r.p. designs they are almost non-existent. In a wooden boat if you
                  want lace hooks, for example, to make fast a tent cover just below
                  the gunwale you merely screw them on. (Fig. 5.) In a g.r.p. boat
                  this could be a lot less simple.
                     Builders of glass boats seem to pride themselves on the mirrorlike

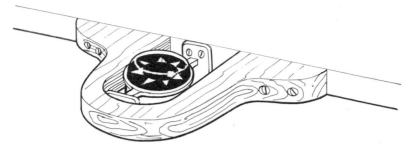

Fig. 6 An arrangement for a steering compass mounted on a stern thwart. In this case the very compact 'Sestrel Junior' has been used.

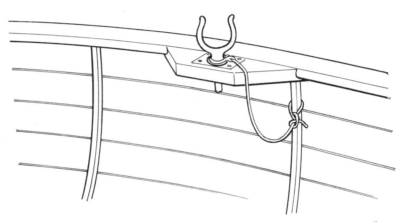

Fig. 7 A reminder that rowlocks should be fitted with lanyards not only to prevent loss but in order to find them quickly from the bottom of the boat.

finish they can bestow, not only on hull exteriors where it is proper, but on seats and coamings, with little apparent thought to the sliding about and lack of hand-hold that all this gloss means.

Grabrails, a place to mount a steering compass (Fig. 6.) or stand a boom crutch, attachment points for rowlock lanyards (Fig. 7.) or a convenient place to stow an outboard motor; these are reasonable requirements in a day-sailing boat, and I don't know which is worse, the idea that the designer did not foresee the need for them, or that the builder did not think it worthwhile to make provision for them.

Cruising dinghies have a hard life. They have to take the ground on pebble-strewn shores. This means stout bilge rubbing pieces, preferably of wood, are necessary to take the worst of the knocks. Glass fibre can soon look ghastly if it is subject to this sort of treatment without protection—as is too often the case. (Fig. 8.)

**Home
Completion**
Compared with the great deal of thought that goes into detail aboard even small yachts, many glass fibre dinghies positively discourage the owner's interest in tailoring the interior to his own way of working. One ray of hope is that an increasing number of builders are offering bare glass hulls for home completion. Work on these, if the flexible bare hull is properly chocked and supported level before interior joinery is fitted, should be comparatively simple to anybody handy with woodworking tools, and especially anybody who has tackled an all-wood dinghy from a kit. I should make it clear that when I referred to tailoring a boat to the owner's own

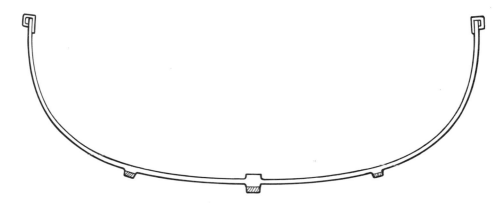

Fig. 8   Section of g.r.p. hull showing addition of wooden keel pieces and bilge rubbers to prevent damaging the gel coat.

requirements, I meant of course that this should be in line with accepted boat-building practice. I once met an optimist who thought of leaving out the thwarts of an open boat to make more room. Another who complained that the centreboard case was in the way. It pays to keep bright ideas under your hat until you have a good experience of boats and why they are constructed as they are. Even then, be careful. The conventional is usually the safest and the most workmanlike. Composite boats, with a wooden deck and thwarts and bottom boards are more expensive than the all-g.r.p. versions, where the deck is fitted like a piecrust on to the hull,

Types

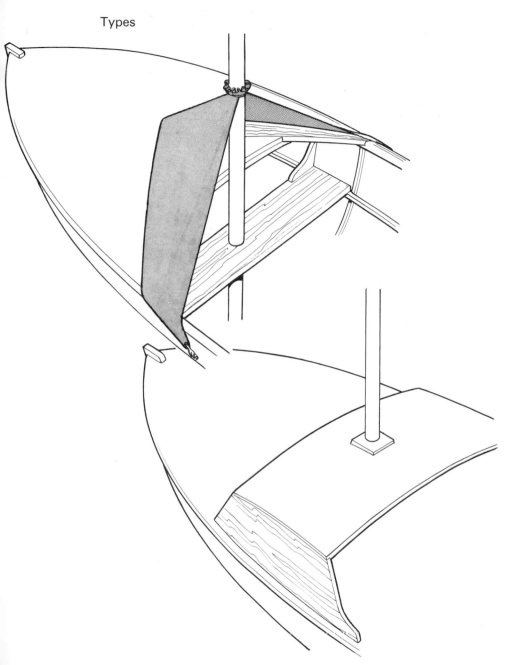

Fig. 9   A comparison of the built on cuddy and a canvas dodger
which can be used when sailing in contrary weather. Built up
structure should be viewed with caution on unballasted boats.

but they have the edge in looks. However they need more maintenance. But you can add bits as you like. In boats of any size, most things are a compromise.

Of course, owners that know best are the bane of the boat-builder's life. The customer, on the other hand, probably thinks that standardization is aimed not so much at keeping costs within bounds as taking the easy way out. Neither view is fair. You can have any colour you like, wily Henry Ford told buyers of his Model T, so long as it's black. The boating branch of the mighty leisure industry has far from reached this take-it-or-leave it stage yet, and I hope it never will.

New Cruisers   Specimen types worth studying in the new wave of dinghy cruisers are the Skipper range from Richmond Marine, the Shipmate, and the Shipmate Senior from Small Craft Ltd. Small Craft it was

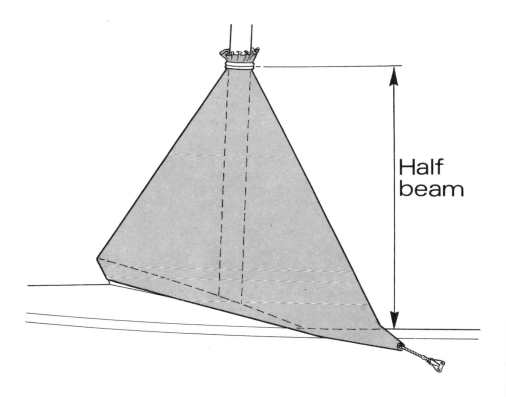

Fig. 10   Another view of a suggested canvas dodger. The height of the collar up the mast should be equal to half the beam of the boat.

Simplicity of rig is a feature of the 12 ft. Skipper by Richmond Marine. She has a roomy dry stowage locker aft for picnic gear, and is something quite different from either the modern racing or traditional wooden dinghy.

who introduced the Wayfarer back in 1957, the most renowned of all modern cruising dinghies and still the most powerful argument against a trend for building small cabins on dinghy hulls and calling them week-end cruisers.

These are inclined to make a dinghy look like a little yacht —a disguise she wears badly—and they rob the dinghy of its valued lightness and roominess for her size. Built-on cuddies (Fig. 9.) are, theoretically, a good idea as somewhere to get out of the rain, but deep water cruising owners like Frank Dye, Talbot Kirk, and others find that a canvas dodger just aft of the foredeck is almost as effective and far less claustrophobic. (Fig. 10.)

A well tailored tent cover which can be extended over the whole boat at the end of a day's sail is more spacious and has the advantage that it can be stowed away when not required, leaving the boat cleared for action. What's more it's cheaper.

To people who have cut their sailing teeth in dinghies and who

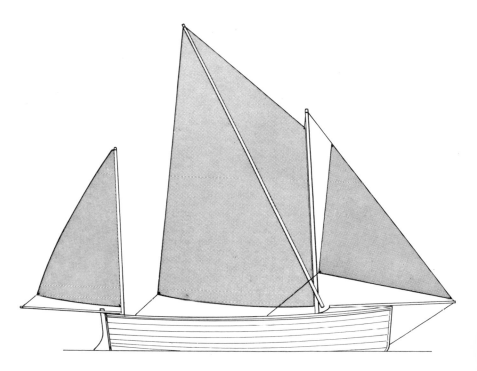

Fig. 11   The sprit rig

realize the importance of their own weight in sailing an unballasted boat, the impression given by the permanent cuddy of lots of top hamper is one not easy to dispel. Cabins are for yachts, I feel,

not for dinghies, which are little fun when they are robbed of their
intrinsic lightness and simplicity. Dinghy cruising means open air,
a dash of spray in your face, simple living, simple sailing, simple
upkeep and transport. You pay in comfort. If you want upholstered
bunks, permanent toilets and gimballed galleys, then look for
something larger than a sixteen foot hull to squeeze them in.

Craft more in the spirit of open-boat sailing with a less
domesticated approach are the Drascombe range, produced in g.r.p.
by Honnor Marine. The largest, the 22-ft. Longboat, while open,
is a bit beyond the size range set for this book. But she, like the
smaller Lugger (18 ft. 9 ins.) and the newcomer to the range,
the Dabber (15 ft. 6 ins.) are thoroughly in the spirit of lightness
and simplicity which I reckon are the paramount attractions of
dinghies.

They are open, with side benches extending around the flat-
floored cockpit, with a well for the outboard motor built in forward
of the transom, so that it can stay clamped on, yet protected,
while the boat sails, built to row when required, with plenty of
space for stowage and with jaunty hulls reminiscent of that sea-
grace so characteristic of Shetland boats or the cobles of the
north-east coast.

What is of special interest in all the Drascombe boats, is their
rig. The Dabber, for instance, which was introduced in 1972, is
yawl rigged, with a sprit mainsail, set loose footed, with a foresail
set on a bowsprit and with a loose footed mizzen which sheets to a
bumkin outboard aft, in the manner of the old sailing fishing craft.

The sailplan is low, probably not as efficient as the Bermudian
or gunter rigs, and the loose-footed main could be a handful off
the wind without some sort of whisker pole to hold it out. But I
would swop a bit of efficiency in a cruising boat for such capable
looking character.

The sprit rig, (Fig. 11.) most familiar on the sailing barges of the
Thames and the Estuary, is probably the oldest known fore-and-aft
rig and was widely popular among open-boat sailors before the
dipping and standing lugs took over. Its most endearing feature is
that it can be furled without lowering it. A brailing line gathers the
sail in against the mast like a curtain, leaving the inside of the boat
uncluttered.

Auxiliary Power   In an open boat, oars and motors are more a part of getting
along than in the cruising yacht, where sail reigns supreme, and the
auxiliary engine is just a necessity for bettering a tide or making
harbour on time. Dinghy sailing in anything of a breeze is wet,
lively work. Because one wants the best possible weather for a
cruise, this means using fine settled weather when calms or light
airs prevail. This is when an outboard motor makes all the difference
to the success of keeping to a cruise schedule. Often along the coast
in summer, anticyclone weather means a long period of hazy calm
during the morning, until the sun heats the land up enough to start
the sea breeze flowing ashore. Without a motor, a cruising dinghy

A roomy cruising boat specially designed for home building is the Mirror 16. It makes a fine medium or long range cruising dinghy. LOA 16 ft., beam 6 ft., draft 6 in., with plate down 3 ft. 6 in., weight is 260 lb.

would make poor showing in that calm period. With one she can be well on her way to the next port of call and still enjoy good sailing later in the day.

   In a dinghy the safest way of getting along in the conditions of the moment is the proper one, be it under engine, oars or sails. As a good dinghy should be equally happy under any of the three, there is no need to be purist about the superiority of sail over auxiliary power. It can be safer to run for shelter under motor with the sails stowed, and handier to row instead of sail through the

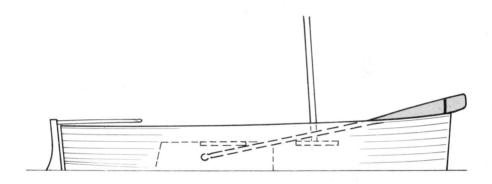

Fig. 12   It is better for oars to project beyond the boat when stowed, rather than be too short for comfortable rowing. Here they are shown stowed each side of the centreboard case with the blades forward.

crowded moorings of a busy harbour. After a long day in an open boat, it is far more satisfactory to arrive than to travel hopefully.

   Engines are smelly, noisy intruders into open boat sailing, but all is forgiven when the wind fails, leaving the boat a mile from her destination and with the tide beginning to turn foul. The only reason I can think of for not shipping an outboard on a cruise would be the problems of space. This applies particularly in a boat of twelve feet or less. Clamping the monster on the conventional transom of a boat of this size can also be a delicate performance if there is any lop left on the sea. For a really small dinghy there is everything in favour of a pair of oars as standby power.

Oars Should Be Long

   Oars have dropped out of favour in small boats mainly because people will buy them too short. One can row a twelve footer for hours with a pair of oars of between seven and eight feet, using long and leisurely strokes. Shorter oars are easier to stow in the boat and they cost less, but they are awkward to use.

They need quicker strokes, causing the rower to bend his arms instead of rowing from the waist with his arms straight. He tires in no time and thereafter condemns rowing as a means of getting along, when in fact it is the most convenient and auxiliary power there is. To buy oars according to the most convenient length for stowage is to miss the point. Let the blades overhang the transom or the bow if they must, with the looms tucked under the main thwart. (Fig. 12.) This will keep the ends from snarling sheets and halyards and protect them from being trodden or sat upon—the most

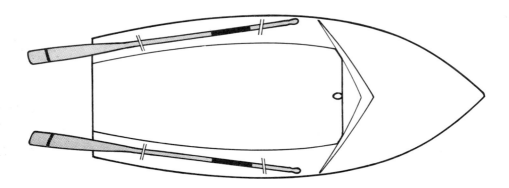

Fig. 13   Oars stowed on side decks using lashings : in this case they overhang the transom.

common fate for breakables in dinghies. In a half-decked boat, small chocks can be fastened to the coamings or side decks so that the oars may be made fast there with shock cord or lanyards when not in use. (Fig. 13.) I suggest the crew makes a habit of stowing the oars with the blades at the stern of the boat. In this way the rower brings the oar towards the rowlock without having to reverse it, with less risk of fouling shrouds or halyards or of braining the crew.

Decking   As for decking, it can be overdone in an ordinary dinghy. Assuming that she is not of the self-draining type, (which is not likely to make a successful cruising dinghy,) any water that comes

Types

The traditional open-boat rig of sprit mainsail and loose-footed
mizzen was revived for the 15 ft. Drascombe Dabber, introduced
in 1972. The hull is glass fibre, with simulated clinker strakes.

The 12 ft. mahogany clinker Tideway Class dinghy—an ideal all-purpose seaboat, and still a best-seller despite rivalry from glass fibre.

aboard will have to be shifted by self-bailers (if the boat has the speed potential to help them work properly) or by old-fashioned pumping and bailing. Any decent sailing breeze means that spray will be coming aboard over the weather bow. It is inevitable, and

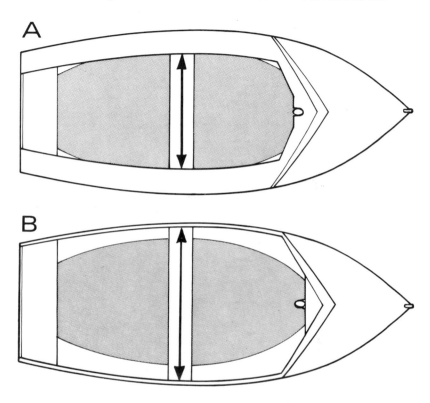

Fig. 14   Side decking is a debatable point in a twelve foot boat. The decked boat has better sitting but less leg room, A; on the other boat the crew has to sit on the gunwale, but does not have to move out so early as the thwarts are available at extremity, B. Measurements show different proportions.

harmless if put back again as soon as possible.

A good area of foredeck, especially if fitted with deep washboards, keeps some out, but is chiefly valuable for protecting gear stowed forward out of the way. But most spray flies in abaft the mast anyway. Side decks do little more than provide a comfortable seat for sitting out, but then so does the plain gunwale of an undecked boat. In a boat of twelve feet or less, side decks take up too much room to be justified. (Fig. 14.)

One of the dangerous fallacies about side decks is that they

allow the boat to be sailed at a greater degree of heel without
shipping water over the lee side. She is badly sailed if she has
to rely on that. As for high coamings inboard of the side decks,
these are old fashioned yacht fittings scaled down to dinghy size by

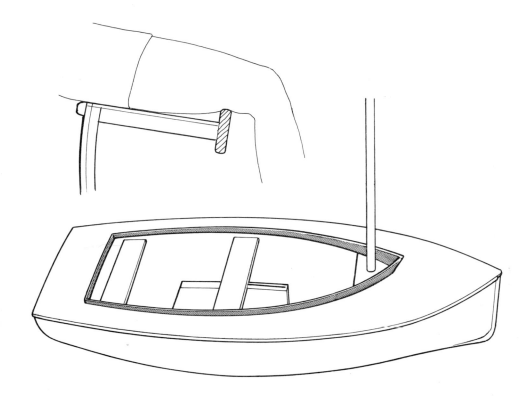

Fig. 15   The side deck problem in three dimensions. Coamings
keep out some deck surface water, but are inconvenient when
sitting out.

builders who don't sail dinghies themselves, or they would realize
how abominably uncomfortable they are to sit on when driving the
boat to windward. (Fig. 15.)

Toestraps   Any centreboarder goes better if the crew can get their weight
as far up to windward as possible. (Fig. 16.) Therefore, it is useful to
have toe straps of some sort on the boat. These have to be more of
a compromise than in a racing boat, because they can get in the way

of stowage or sleeping bodies. Even a slow, heavy boat becomes more fun if her crew can sit well out and drive her. Conversely, there is nothing in dinghy sailing more ignominious than having to spill the mainsheet in a good sailing breeze because the human weight aboard cannot be shifted to the best position.

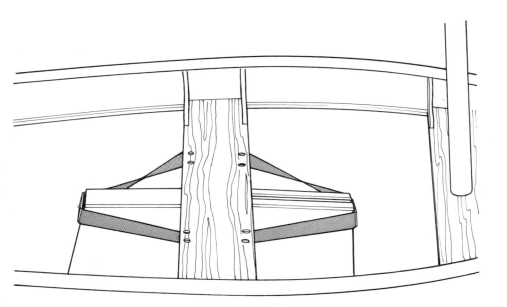

Fig. 16   Toestraps are essential to efficient sailing. They can be screwed, or bolted where necessary, to thwart and centreboard.

Sitting Out   Side decks, besides being in the way most of the time, tend to encourage people to sit comfortably with their bottoms inboard. The gunwale of an open boat encourages a more outboard position, with the weight taken at the tops of the legs. I have sailed an undecked dinghy to windward for hours, sitting this way on a gunwale capping just over two inches wide without discomfort. It is usually the abdomen muscles and those of the mainsheet gripping hand that begin to complain long before those one is sitting on.

In a dinghy travelling at a good speed, the water streaming past her deeply immersed lee side is little to be concerned about. When she heels too far and overbalances towards a capsize, the water that pours in over the lee side is the effect of the tumble rather than its cause. A capsize in a cruising dinghy is a serious business and incidentally is the most important reason for having a boat small enough for the crew to right if it happens. But, as an experiment, it is

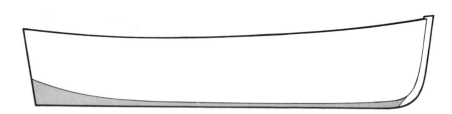

Fig. 17   Profile of cruising dinghy which retains skeg, with several advantages over rocker bottom type racing hull

worth getting a boat sailing full and fast and gradually letting her bear away, keeping the sheets in, but not made fast. As she heels more, the motion of the boat tends to push the water out of the way so that the gunwale can appear to run several inches below the true surface before this deflected wave collapses and falls inboard.

Charles Sandison describes how this was a well-known characteristic of sailing the Shetland Sixerns. In these low, lean Viking-type boats, the knowledge that with plenty of way on she was less likely to swamp must have been comforting for the crews who sailed miles into the Atlantic without the benefit of decking.

Straight Keel and Skeg   Old fashioned boats were built with a long straight keel, with the line of this developed into a skeg where the planking ran up towards the transom. This has become obsolete in racing dinghies in the quest to reduce wetted surface and to make the boat quicker in stays. (Fig. 17.) But in cruising, a boat with a skeg has some

advantages. It is inclined to make her run truer downwind, will
certainly row better than a boat with no grip on the water and will
sail in shallow water with far less centreboard down than a rocker-
bottomed racing dinghy would tolerate. What is more, she will
heave to, leaving the crew free to tuck in a reef, check position or
take a quick snack. A boat that is too lively can be as tedious as one
that is too sluggardly in the cruising game. One that does not
require constant attention under way helps save the crew from
fatigue, with all its evil consequences; from bad temper, at the least,
or more serious errors such as to misreading the flashes of a light
on the approach to a strange harbour in bad visibility.

4 Boat sense

Cruising in small open boats does not require great proficiency in the higher arts of seamanship. For a boat that floats in a few inches of water, chartwork is an academic, rather than urgent practical interest; meteorology involves none of the laborious plotting of fronts and systems which offshore sailors are heir to—when in any doubt about the weather, don't go. A few simple knots and the ability to whip a rope's end, or turn an eye splice in replacement sheets or halyards is most of the essential marline-spike seamanship.

Good reflexes, cool nerves and sensitive powers of observation are worth more to the dinghy sailor than all the manifold arts listed in the Department of Trade and Industry Yachtmaster's Examination. You need no instruments apart from a compass or—later on, when a higher standard of proficiency has been reached—a direction-finding radio. The main requirement is an intimate rapport with and confidence in the boat.

I suggested the choice of a boat light enough to be kept ashore when she is not in use. But a mooring is the obvious answer for a heavier boat which needs a team of helpers to haul her up and down a slipway. Small boats on moorings, however, need watching, bailing out after heavy rain and scrubbing off during the summer months when the weed and scum are at their most virile.

Getting to and from a boat on moorings means a tender is necessary, which pushes your overheads up before you get anywhere. So does the mooring itself for which most harbour authorities impose a charge, albeit modest. Another point to remember is that despite all the admirable work done by police and harbour masters to reduce the menace, vandalism is an increasing risk for boats left afloat unattended.

Non-Slip Coatings
The sartorial care lavished on racing boats is out of place in one that cruises. A cruising owner will see a varnished fore-deck not in terms of its beautiful gloss, but on his chances of survival if he had to stand on it, hauling on an anchor warp in a lively sea. On his own boat he has probably sacrificed shine for security and coated

it with non-slip paint or sand-sprinkled varnish.

Compared with her racing sister, the cruising dinghy is a workboat, in which finish is judged not by how it looks but how it keeps the weather out of the fabric. But as anybody knows who has visited a harbour used by inshore fishermen, a boat that does a rough job does not have to look rough. Pilot cutters, tugs and customs launches are often beautifully maintained, without giving the visitor

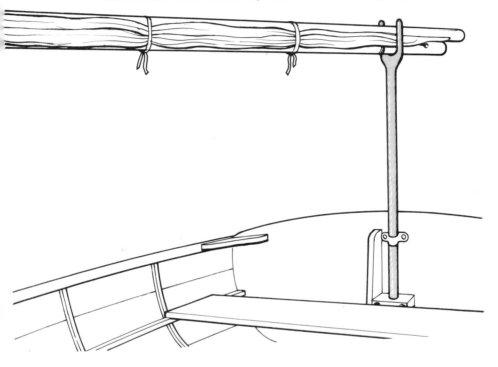

Fig. 18 Arrangement for boom crutch and mainsail stowage. Sail is flaked between boom and gaff and then lashed with tiers.

the idea that he would be unwelcome aboard in anything but rubber-soled shoes.

For woodwork, paint is probably more durable than conventional varnish, although the two-can polyurethanes are marvellously tough. On a g.r.p. boat with wood trim, the texture of wood under varnish does wonders to relieve the blank look of the plastic surface, and in wooden boats varnish has the advantage of revealing saturation and other latent deterioration in the wood.

Varnish touches up better than paint after a knock, and a new preparation for making this job easier is moisture-cured polyurethane, in which the moisture content of the air acts as a hardener. When using polyurethanes, remember to have a can of the maker's thinners handy for cleaning the brush.

Sails and gear have a tough life in a cruising boat. The racing owner unbends his sails after every race, rinses them in fresh water and, after drying them, folds them away very carefully so that the creases run in the direction of the air-flow when the sail is in use. In a cruising dinghy, the sails are commonly bent on the spars at

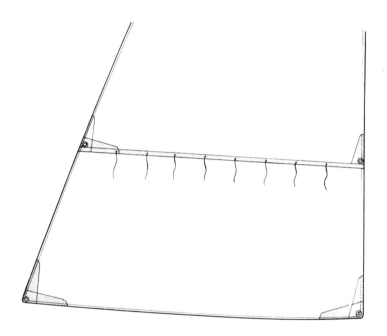

Fig. 19   Sailmakers are used to making light sails for dinghies. Extra reinforcement is needed for cruising boats including tabling at cringles and strengthened seam at reef point line.

the beginning of the season, and left there until the end, salt and all.

The main can be rolled and secured with tiers when the boom rests in a boom crutch, (Fig. 18.) or loosely flaked down when the boom is laid along the benches inside. In my twelve footer, in which the mast is lowered to serve as ridgepole for the waterproof cover, I leave the jib bent to the halyard for quicker getaway from the launching place. Wonderful rot-proof Terylene makes such neglect possible.

Avoid Sail Battens

Battens are a menace in cruising boat sails. They are too easily trodden on and broken when the main is lowered, and the top one of the conventional three, which is the most useless one of them all, has to be removed to get a smooth sausage when the sail is furled along the boom. Terylene is so stable that the risk of distortion and

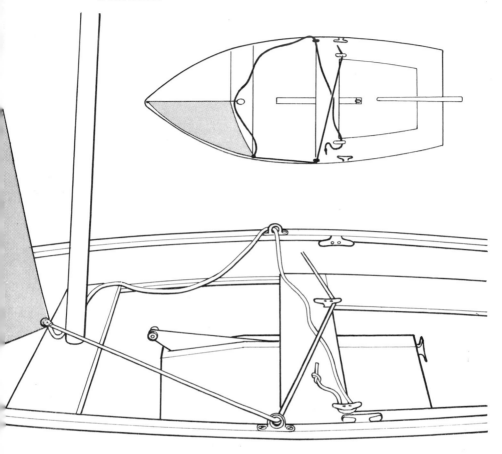

Fig. 20   Suitable cleat and lead positions

stretching are minimal compared with cotton, but to avoid the risk of abusing a good sail it is worthwhile asking the advice of a sailmaker to see if straightening the leech, whereby the sail loses only an insignificant part of its area, might be a way of dispensing with battens.

Sails for cruising boats can be cheaper. Second-hand racing suits are available regularly and a sailmaker—generally he is one of the most approachable of men in the sailing business—will make alterations, such as sewing in a row of reef points or strengthening the tabling at the corners and cringles to prepare them for the tougher cruising life. (Fig. 19.)

Shrouds need be only galvanized wire. Stainless is an unnecessary luxury. In a cruising boat there is no need to be concerned with excess windage, so the shrouds should be made twice as thick, or at least half as thick again as those specified for a racing boat of comparable overall length. The galvanizing lasts much longer on thicker wire and thicker shrouds are stronger.

Preserving Wire

To preserve galvanized wire, it should be dressed with boiled linseed oil, warmed to make it runny and more penetrating. A useful memory aid for buying the correct oil is that boiled linseed like boiled milk, leaves a skin; raw (for use on bare wood) soaks in.

A sound safety move in dinghies is to position leads and cleats of running rigging so that as many jobs as possible can be done from where the crew is sitting. (Fig. 20.) Under most conditions a boat will lie quietly head to wind under main alone. The halyard for the main can therefore be cleated in the normal way at or near the foot of the mast. After all, having to dowse the main while the boat is romping along would be virtually impossible. She would turn up into the wind by herself anyway.

With the jib it is different. When a squall threatens or when the boat is approaching a crowded slipway, with other craft about the helmsman would be glad to get the jib off her quickly while still keeping her sailing, to improve his visibility and to make her handier. The jib halyard, therefore, should be led aft and cleated somewhere within reach of the helmsman's steering position (Fig. 21.) on the centreboard case or the main thwart, perhaps, where it can be cast off with one hand.

Jib Downhaul

To ensure that the sail comes down smartly when the halyard (Fig. 22) is cast off, one end of a piece of thin line can be made fast to the head eyelet of the sail, led through the piston hanks or slides parallel with the forestay, through the shackle at the foot of the sail and thence aft, again to a convenient point within reach. When the halyard is cast off, this downhaul can tug the jib down into a neat bundle at the foot of the stay, and prevents it riding up again and flapping, as it will do in anything of a breeze.

Even in the smallest dinghy it is sometimes handier to pick up a spare mooring on a short visit. This is even more tricky in a single-handed dinghy that is aboard a heavier boat, because of the principle of the mat on the slippery floor—as you walk forward it slides back. So does a light boat, as you go forward to bring in the mooring buoy over the bow.

Mooring Hook

Any operation which keeps one away from the helm too long aboard a dinghy with sail set is not welcome, especially in a busy harbour. A useful piece of gear to make the job easier is an updated version of the West Country mooring hook, which Conor O'Brien describes in his Book 'the Sea Boat'.

A hook, if it is to be deep-mouthed enough to reduce the risk of slipping free, will be heavy, so a large spring hook is preferable. (Fig. 23) Not one of the expensive Swedish stainless steel types, but a galvanized one, with a leaf spring, a larger version of the clip used on a dogs lead. Make this fast to a piece of stout line, sufficiently long to bring the hook aft to the helmsman when the other end is made fast to the ringbolt or mooring cleat. Sail slowly up to the mooring to bring it amidships, clip the hook to the grab loop on the buoy, and this will stop her drifting away until the mooring is brought aboard properly.

Anchors   When cruising, you need a good anchor aboard. Not one of the tiny toys which are just heavy enough to hold a racing dinghy over the ground in a calm, but the biggest which will stow

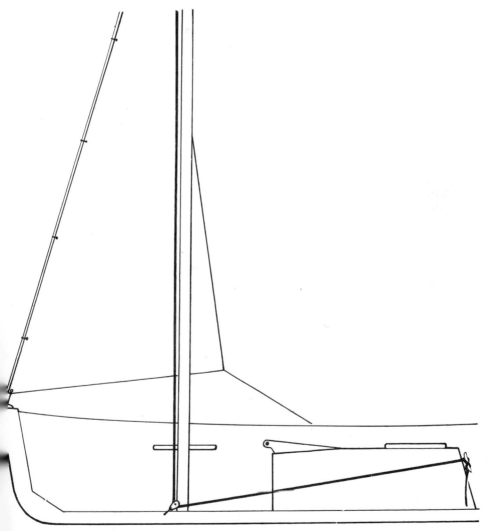

Fig. 21   It must be possible to drop the jib quickly and halyard should be led aft and cleated within reach of the helmsman.

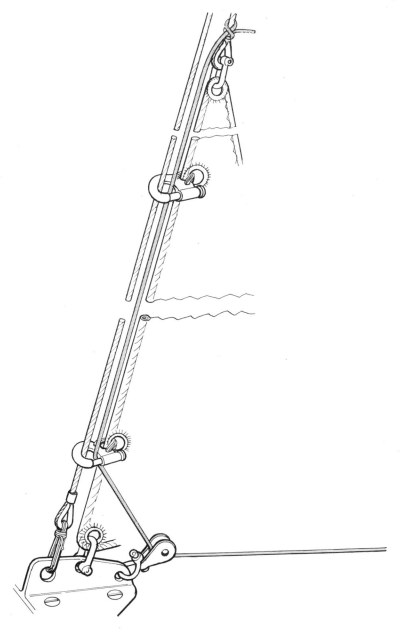

Fig. 22   It is not possible to stand or even sit on the foredeck to ensure the headsail comes down : so instead a jib downhaul should be used.

conveniently, (Fig. 24) which can be relied upon to hold her off a lee shore in any sort of dinghy weather.

Fisherman pattern anchors have only one advantage over modern types; the stock can be folded flush with the shank to give a neat stow. But the Fisherman is the devil to prepare because of that sliding stock. The locking pin, which is supposed to hold the stock central in the crown, invariably fits badly and falls out—sometimes, if one is unlucky, below the surface and undetected until the anchor starts to drag.

A stockless anchor, then, is a better choice. Weight for weight it is supposed to be more efficient than a fisherman, but I think this has more to do with the nature of the bottom than the design alone. For a boat between twelve and fourteen feet which has to rely on an anchor during a cruise or a week-end away, a ten pound

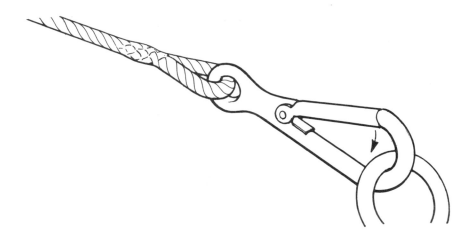

Fig. 23 Mooring hook enables line to be secured quickly to a buoy, as it may not be possible to lean over the gunwale long enough to make fast.

C.Q.R. type is a good working size. For extra efficiency, shackle a fathom or more of $\frac{3}{16}$ inch chain between the anchor and the warp, primarily to make the pull of the warp horizontal instead of upward and also to relieve the warp of chafe on the bottom.

Before sailing on after anchoring, it is worth a bit of time to coil down the anchor warp as nearly as possible and tie the coil neatly, using shoelace knots, with two or three pieces of light line. Nothing is a more desperate mess nor a surer sign of trouble than ten fathoms of warp in a tangle when a boat needs to anchor quickly.

**Smooth
Running
Coils**
Blame for halyards or sheets that will not stay free for running usually lies in the inadequate cleating arrangements in many modern dinghies. A cleat should have a long enough horn to take an extra turn which can hold the coiled fall of the halyard. Tucking the coil between a taut standing part and the mast looks neat—

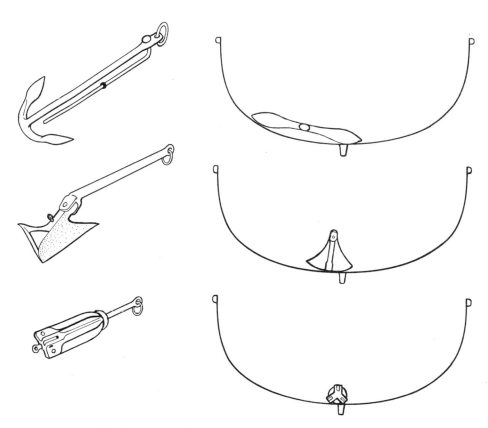

Fig. 24   The problems of anchor stowage

until the time comes to move it and it becomes an enormous knot.
    If the fall can hang from the cleat in a neat coil, or can be laid on the bottom boards, bitter-end downwards, before casting off, it should run without snagging. (Fig. 25) Nothing can really be said to work properly in a dinghy unless it works well when the crew are ham-fisted with tiredness, or are all fingers and thumbs in the excitement of an emergency. If an old-fashioned fitting works better than a modern variant, then it deserves its place. Never mind if it is heavy or lacks 'styling'.

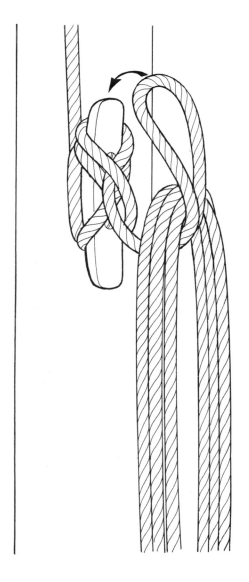

Fig. 25   Methods of stowing halyards

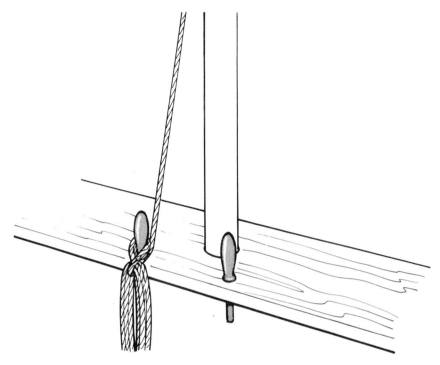

Fig. 26   Belaying pins used for halyards when the mast is stepped through a thwart

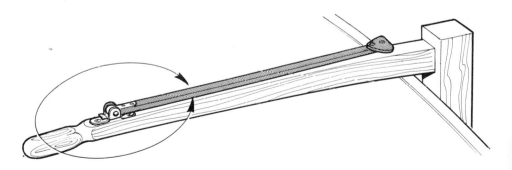

Fig. 27   Tiller extension enables steering to be far less tiring. Hinge should avoid the end of tiller to allow ordinary steering from that point. Handle ends should be sanded and unvarnished.

Belaying Pins   I make up my halyards on to small belaying pins mounted in the aft side of the mast thwart. (Fig. 26) They grip a halyard with only half the number of turns a slippery nylon cleat requires and, because of their larger diameter, they cast off much more sweetly. They look good as well.

Just as toe straps have their place in a cruising dinghy, so does a tiller extension, (Fig. 27) without which the helmsman cannot exert his weight outboard to the best advantage. One should not have to lay out like a trapeze man in a cruising boat. But merely sitting up on the weather gunwale, without any more athletics, makes the world of difference to a boat's performance to windward.

Bottom boards, and any surface where it is normal to walk— and this includes the foredeck in a larger boat—should be coated in a non-slip material. (Fig. 28) The g.r.p. practice of moulding in the pattern of a non-slip surface is widespread because it is easier to do than to apply a non-slip surface by hand. Too often it is simply not non-slip.

A true skidproof surface does not look elegant. But that is not its concern. If the bottom boards and decking are of wood, the old method of sprinkling fine white sand over a wet coat of varnish, and then overcoating the sand again when the first coat is dry, is a cheap and long lasting method. But the varnish must have time to harden and cure before the surface is walked on, or it won't last a week.

Pumice powder used to be sold for this job by paint dealers, but sand blends with the colour of varnish and wood better. That second coat of varnish is important, by the way. Without it the surface will be as abrasive as sandpaper—which it is, of course. With it, the sharp grit is blunted enough to give trouser bottoms, shoes and sleeping bags a fair chance. Handgrips of tiller and extension should be left bare wood, gently roughed up once a season with coarse sandpaper. This will give sufficient grip, even for a cold wet hand.

Fenders and Warps   Useful items of gear on a cruise are a set of small fenders, two or more of them, to protect the boat if she has to lie alongside another craft or a pontoon in a harbour. Cowes is an example of where this is nearly always necessary. Good warps are essential, no matter what the size of the boat. That used as anchor warp should be good and long. About 14 fathoms of 1-in. or $\frac{3}{4}$-in. circumference Terylene might seem an expensive outlay, but if well used it will last for years. A warp of this length is useful too if the boat has to lie off a quay wall, when at low water the top of the quay may be twenty or thirty feet overhead. Remember also that a stern warp is necessary. This too should be of ample length and strength, and have its own well fastened attachment at the stern. Lying alongside anything, boat or pontoon, is not a happy situation for a cruising dinghy. Compared with larger boat she is so lively that the wash from passing traffic will set her dancing, cause her to bump and surge distressingly. That is where those fenders will prove valuable.

The open boat's greatest asset is that she can be hauled up the
corner of a slip or left to dry on the mud while the crew go ashore
for a couple of hours. In this case it is always wise, in a harbour,
or where there is nobody to keep an eye on the boat, to erect the

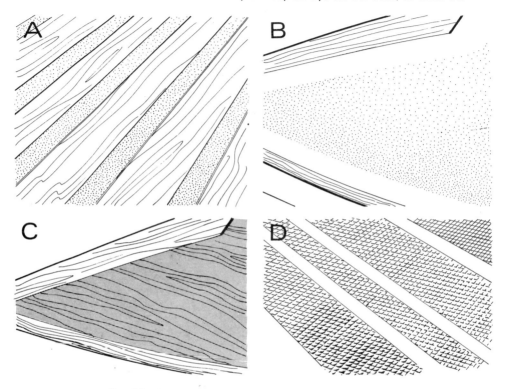

Fig. 28 Non-slip surfaces are important and can be of various
types. Bottom boards and foredeck are the most necessary areas to
be treated in this way.
(a) 'Safety-walk' strips
(b) Sanded paint or varnish
(c) Bare wood
(d) Stick-on plastic patterns

**Helpful
Harbour-
Masters**

tent cover before leaving her. Nobody can complain if gear is
stolen from a boat when it is left exposed to the attention of pilferers.

First job of the skipper after arriving in a harbour should be to call
on the harbourmaster, who can almost always suggest a comfortable
berth which a stranger might not find for himself, and will probably
recommend a boatman who will keep an eye on the boat while her
crew is away. Always play fair and pay up any harbour dues that

are required. For a dinghy these are likely to be so small that evasion is not only petty but unwise, because it disqualifies you from the help of the harbourmaster which is so important to a visitor. At sea, you are on your own, and can have confidence in your self-reliance to cope with situations. Ashore, or in harbour, you cannot have too many friends who understand the needs of small boats and their crews.

Sampson Post

A fitting often neglected on small boats is the strong point to which the mooring rope or anchor chain is made fast. On an open boat, the old method was to have a galvanized ringbolt rivetted into the thick wood of the stem and apron right at the bows. In a boat with a foredeck, the best method is a sampson post, (Fig. 29) a

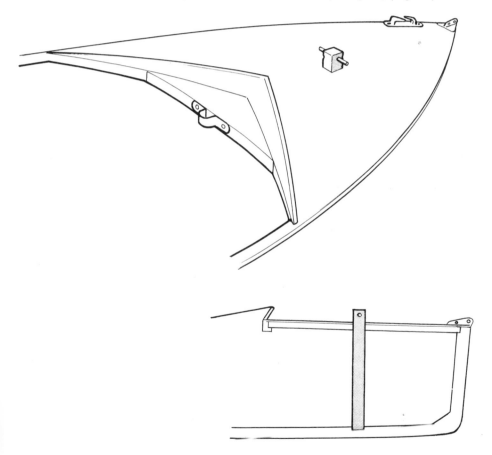

Fig. 29   Sampson post on dinghy foredeck. The principle is that the post passes right down to the keel. This is seen less and less today, but is a sure arrangement.

stout column of wood, stepped into a socket on the hog and
standing up through the foredeck for several inches. Compared with
the silly little cleats, fastened with two brass screws, which pass for
a mooring cleat on some boats today, the sampson post was sturdy
and spread the strain of the tugging mooring line through the fabric
of the boat. A sampson post can be made by screwing or setting in
with glass fibre and resin a block of wood on the keel, socketed to
take the foot of the post and cutting a square hole in the deck to
take the top part. The step for the foot should be positioned after
cutting the deck so that it can be positioned plumb under the hole.
The best place for a post is immediately abaft a deck beam, so that
this can help to take the forward strain.

It is important to have the top of the post sticking up a good
distance from the deck surface—six inches is not too much even in
a small dinghy, because this enables a satisfactory number of turns
to be made. If the mooring is chain, this needs plenty of room to
make fast safely. Another advantage of a good high post is that you
can fit a bronze rod athwartships through the head of it to stop the
mooring riding off of it when the motion is lively.

Ring Bolt

The ring bolt is as sound and seamanlike for open boats as the
sampson post is for decked ones. The anchor rope or long painter
should never be spliced direct to it. A knot, preferably a round turn
and two half hitches, should be used. Otherwise, when the boat is
riding to anchor, there is no way of slipping the warp or making
fast another line to it to give a longer scope. It is a good rule
when under way to unbend the anchor chain from the warp and
lash the anchor separately. This makes for a tidier stow, leaves
the warp ready for use as, say a towline or a long painter, and
prevents the boat anchoring herself if the anchor goes over the side
during a capsize—a dicey situation if a strong tide is running and
the crew are swept away from her.

**Kicking
Straps**

Avoid kicking straps on the boom like the plague. However
useful one may be for giving a racing dinghy a slight increase of
speed by holding the mainsail flat, they are the devil's invention
in crowded cruising boats.

On the wind a kicking strap is not wanted anyway. When running,
the boom can be kept from rising up dangerously by not sailing
dead before the wind (racing helmsmen have to do this, the
shortest distance between two marks being a straight line, but
cruisers can afford to take longer). Instead the course downwind
should be in a slight zig-zag. Stay her round at the end of each leg
if you are confident that she will come round in the state of the sea.
But usually it is better to be bold and gybe.

A cruising boat's gybe is different from that of a racer. The latter
puts course keeping first and, with a kicking strap, the boom
comes over reasonably quietly. A cruising helmsman should forget
such niceties. Let him bring the tiller over slowly but boldly with the
boom sheeted right out so that when it changes sides the mainsail

Boat sense

The shape of a good seaboat is ageless. This one, built by George Feltham of Old Portsmouth in 1967, with her full sections and good freeboard forward, has several open-water passages to her credit.

flags out to leeward, leaving the boat unpressed. She will lose little speed in the short time it takes to get sailing again on the other gybe.

In heavier weather, when the main is reefed, the need for a kicking strap is even less, because the reduced height of the sail makes it even more docile with this gybing drill. When running, lift the centreboard almost to its full extent or the boat could trip over it and capsize if she starts to broach. Get the crew weight right aft—you are not racing, so there is not need to think about the extra transom drag—this will keep the bow buoyant and give the rudder, the blade of which should be right down, more bite in the water.

The curse of gybing is indecision on the helmsman's part. Too often he hopes to get away without putting the boom over, sails more and more by the lee until the main flips over and takes him by surprise. In a laden cruising dinghy this is more dangerous than in a racing boat manned by an agile crew who have room to change side quickly. Always gybe in good time, so that a smooth between seas can be chosen.

A gybe carried out with boldness and decision is far less dangerous than one forced on the helmsman because he has timidly put it off.

5 Sails and Rig

Simplicity in a cruising dinghy's rig should come before efficiency in the scientific racing sense. The theory of what makes boat sails work is well known and students of the art will find it in great detail in most sailing primers, complete with diagrams. It seems sufficient here just to outline the basic features of a rig which is easy to maintain and repair, which is of adequate strength to withstand the inevitable hard wear of cruising (no harder than racing, perhaps, but a racing skipper can be sure of getting replacements quickly. A cruising man cannot), which has easy access to all the running parts, which relies on short spars and shroud lanyards rather than rigging screws, and which can be sailed single handed. Inevitably this leads back to the old working boat rigs which began to die out about fifty years ago. Today, we are so accustomed to rigging dinghies like scaled-down yachts that we sometimes fail to realize that they are not.

In sailing, and especially in cruising, there is not harm in a bit of individuality. Nothing makes a boat more interesting to look at than a breakaway from the invariable Bermudian triangle. In a dinghy, provided the hull shape is conventional, one can have fun at little cost in experimenting with rigs and sailplans. The old open boat rigs were splendid for their purpose, and I'm sure that there are enough good designers who could turn a closer study of them to good account in terms of modern materials.

Variety of Rigs

Open boats are not yachts. I seem to keep on saying that, but it cannot be said too often. The wealth of open-boat rig detail preserved in such classic books as Sir Alan Moore's 'Last Days of Mast and Sail', Edgar March's 'Inshore Craft of Britain in the Days of Sail and Oar' or the catalogue and list of plans of fishing boats and coastal craft published by the Science Museum, London, to name three sources of reference currently available, show how much there is to go on. In these days of mass-produced boats, owners are embellishing their boats with gilded carvings and other ornaments to try and achieve individuality, when the most romantic stroke of all would be to set up a new rig. What you have to avoid is being

'picturesque.' It is true as ever that what works right in a boat
will look right. Sails and spars are just machines, after all.

A boat which sails satisfactorily under one sail should never be
given two just to make her look more yachty, or more conventional
in the racing dinghy sense. It is a pity that the standing lug (Fig. 30)

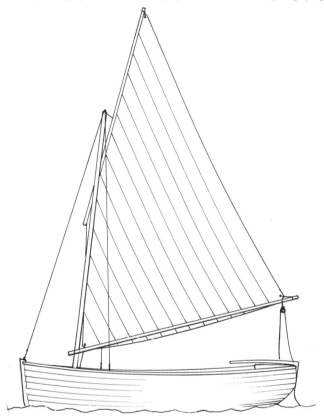

Fig. 30   Standing lug, note rake of mast

has lost favour, mainly because racing has made it seem that the
prime art of boat sailing is getting to windward faster than anybody
else. The cruising man, although glad of a boat that will drive well to
windward when occasion demands it, will soon learn that handiness
in stowing and setting sail is far more important, especially in
open boats, and in this the standing lug was supreme. If ever a
boat owner wanted to turn his hand to sailmaking, incidentally, the
standing lug is the best one for the novice to tackle. But that's
another story, outside the scope of this book.

In a small open boat two shrouds and a forestay are all the
rigging one should need. In the old standing lug-rigged boats the
masts were stouter spars than we know today, and they had no

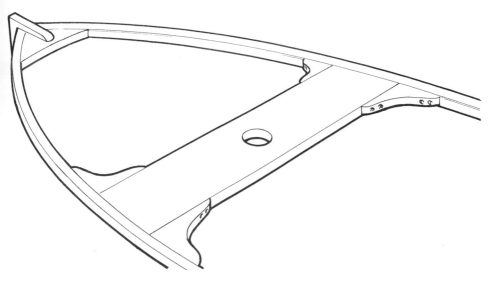

Fig. 31   Mast clamp for standing lug and similar rigs

standing rigging at all, just the halyard, which, as it came back down from the masthead, passed through an eye right in the stem and thus acted as a forestay to counteract the backward pull of the sheet.

The short mast, provided it was set into a stout clamp (Fig. 31) or thwart was saved from too much sideways strain by the heel of the boat in a heavier puff.

Conventional Rig

So, if any alterations are planned for a cruising dinghy's rig, let them be based on a clear knowledge of what sort of boat she is—an open, unballasted boat. In a second-hand dinghy which has a conventional sloop rig, either Bermudian or gunter, the owner should not be in a hurry to alter it if it works well. After all, most outstanding dinghy voyages of recent years have sailed under such rigs.

One has to compromise. There is no denying that a modern rig is better to windward, and we all have to go to windward sometimes. A rig which has windward qualities and yet still many of the advantages of the lugsail is the gunter lug. A traditional sprit-rigged or standing lug-rigged boat is always a joy to see, but match her performance to windward against your own more uniform, less glamourous rig, before you think seriously about emulating her dashing appearance.

Old time sail plans were right for open boats in one vital respect. They were lower, and because the sails were set without a boom along the foot they were less pressing. Chief of all the things which most disturbed the old boatmen when Bermudian rig became

The door of an aft locker should be hinged at its bottom edge to prevent gear spilling out as it is opened.

widespread, was the notion of the foot of the mainsail laced straight and lifeless to the boom. I set the mainsails of my two dinghies on a boom, but unlaced, (Fig. 32) and there seems to be more drive and lift lower down the sail, because the aerofoil curve is maintained down the whole leading edge instead of ending in that dead looking straight line. Both these mains are reefed by reefing points in the old-fashioned way, and the loose-footed setting makes this job easier and quicker.

Dowsing the Jib   In a cruising boat, particularly one sailed single-handed, the jib can be dowsed when the wind is anywhere free. Going to windward

without a jib can be tedious, slow work, so it should always be bent
on ready for use. It is bad practice to think of the jib as the first
reef in a dinghy. Crews often hand it when the boat gets hard-pressed
and then are afraid to set it again when they need it most. The best
way is to make sure that the main is reefed to suit the conditions,
always reefed enough to carry the jib in safety, and always reefed

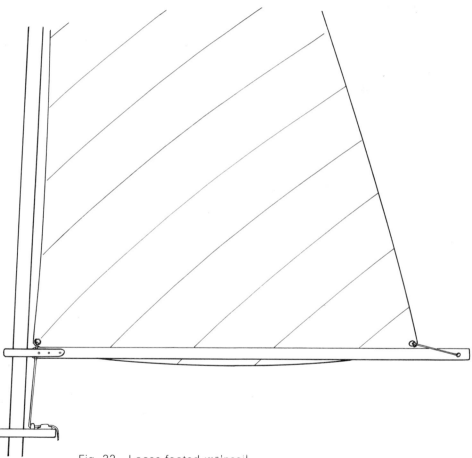

Fig. 32   Loose footed mainsail

in terms of having to go to windward if necessary, even when the
course is a broad reach or a run.

As I mentioned earlier, the choice of suitable dinghies for day
sailing and camping cruising has widened a little in recent years,
after a spell of everything in the dinghy world being tailored
exclusively to racing. This applies to sail plans also, which are
generally smaller and lower than one would demand in racing craft.
Alloy spars are beautifully made today, but I still prefer wood,
especially for a gunter-rigged boat. Not the least of its virtues is
that an owner can repair a break, or even make a new spar without
too much skill.

Spar Making   Many years ago I was heartened to read in an old book that the
making of small spars was one boat-building job that even a
modestly-skilled amateur could tackle. And it is true. One of the
most satisfying woodworking jobs I know is to shape a spar out of
a good piece of sitka spruce (yes, still available if you can shop
around). Anybody, who can handle a plane or a spokeshave can
make a spar. Making a hollow one for a Bermudian rig takes more
skill—and involves a long search for timber long enough for, say, the
mast of a fourteen footer. But when the finished job stands aloft,
gleaming in its new varnish, it's a proud moment.

Short spars as required for boats under fourteen feet are by no
means heavy, and are probably a match for alloy in terms of weight.
A mast for a gunter-rigged boat can be made solid. It needs no
internal groove or slide track and the shrouds, instead of being
shackled to tangs bolted to the sides of the spar merely need looped
ends which lay over a shoulder cut into the masthead. Halyards on a
dinghy up to fourteen feet do not really need wheel sheaves. The
shining texture of pre-stretched Terylene is just right for that old
device, the dumb sheave, (Fig. 33) which is simply a hardwood
fairlead, shaped and grooved like a sheave at the top, but square at
the bottom, so that it sits firmly in the mast slot. In his famous but
now rare book, 'The Sea Boat, How to Build, Rig, and Sail Her,'
R. C. Leslie describes how he fitted dumb sheaves on his sixteen foot
standing-lug rigged yawl. One thing you can be sure of with a dumb
sheave, is that it will not jam. Another advantage is that there is no
sheave pin to pull through the wood under prolonged strain.

Gunter Rig   Another advantage of gunter rig—they'll creep in to this chapter
frequently, I'm afraid—is that the luff of the sail does not have to be
laced or tracked to the mast. Leathered jaws are better and stronger
for the throat end of the gaff than a slide on a track, (Fig. 34)
although this fitting when the sail is set, and the yard almost
vertical, has very little load, most of the strain being taken by
swigging down the luff taut. I have found that the distance of the
luff between the gaff jaws and the tack of the sail is really too short
to require lacing to the mast. There is a lot, I feel, in the old Dutch
idea, that it is better to have the luff standing well clear of the mast
anyway, (Fig. 35) so that it will avoid the spoilt wind it would get

In a larger dinghy a pin rail is useful for making halyards fast. The turns can be cast off quickly and the loose coil will run without snarling.

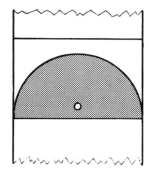
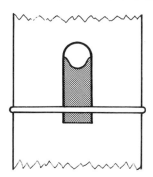

Fig. 33   Dumb sheave : forward and side views

if it were laced or slid on a track. The greatest advantage of this loose-luff method is that, barring a snarled halyard, there is nothing to stop the sail coming down smartly.

If a snap hook is fitted to the parrel balls on the jaws of the gaff, the parrel can be cast off as the sail comes down, so that the sail and spars can be handed forward smartly out of the way. I do not use a gooseneck fitting on the boom. Instead the boom has a pair of wooden jaws and the luff of the sail is bowsed down taut with a tack tackle. (Fig. 36) There are no parrels on the boom jaws because the tension of the luff holds them effectively against the mast.

Boom Jaws   The boom jaws spread the pressure load of the boom against the mast better, they are obviously handier in making and lowering sail, because there are no metal fittings for frozen fingers to have to tinker with, and, most important, anybody with rudimentary carpentry skill can repair a broken jaw. It would need a well equipped machine shop to make a gooseneck fitting if there was no chandlery to buy one from.

Disadvantages   It is only fair to mention in passing some of the disadvantages of the gunter rig. There is slightly more weight aloft, where the gaff and the mast overlap each other, and the gaff, because of its length, takes up a devil of a lot of room when it is lying in the boat. Then there is reefing which, if the yard is hoisted by a single halyard, means lowering the lot and shifting the halyard position (Fig. 37) along the spar when the reef points are tied in. Compared with this the simple rolling of a Bermudian sail around the boom is a luxury, but I do not concede that reefing a Bermudian sail while it is hoisted is safer.

But when it is reefed, the gunter mainsail has virtually shortened the mast by lowering the height of the yard. (Fig. 38) Points reefing, whether on a gunter or Bermudian sail, looks neater and does not impose the torque strain on the gooseneck that roller reefing does, whereby the boom is removed from the square-section gooseneck fitting, the required number of mainsail rolls turned on it, and then socketed back on the fitting.

Points reefing seems to allow a sail to set better. The sail reefed in this way sets flatter—an advantage in heavy weather—whereas a sail rolled up on the boom takes on a ragged look. On yachts fitted with roller reefing gear, this is effectively avoided with one crew member guiding the sail down into neat rolls while another turns the reefing handle. Big boat reefing gear like this would be too large and heavy for use on a dinghy.

In dinghies, one should keep every possible thing simple. And roller reefing on the square ended gooseneck fitting is simple. But I suggest that pulling down a point reef by making the luff and leech eyelets fast to the boom with a few turns of light line, which should

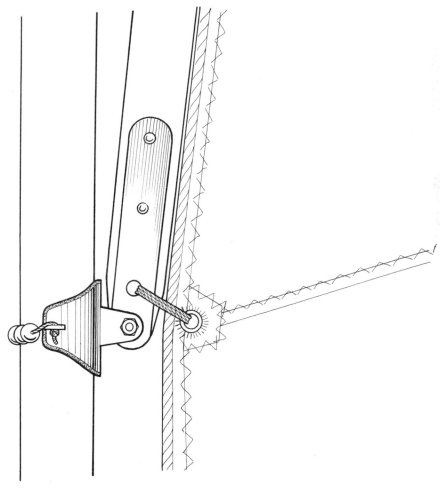

Fig. 34   Head of gunter lug with leather saddle

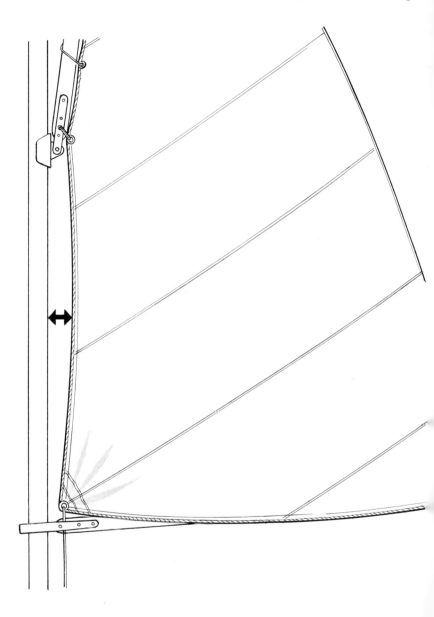

Fig. 35   There is no harm in the luff of the gunter mainsail standing clear of the mast.

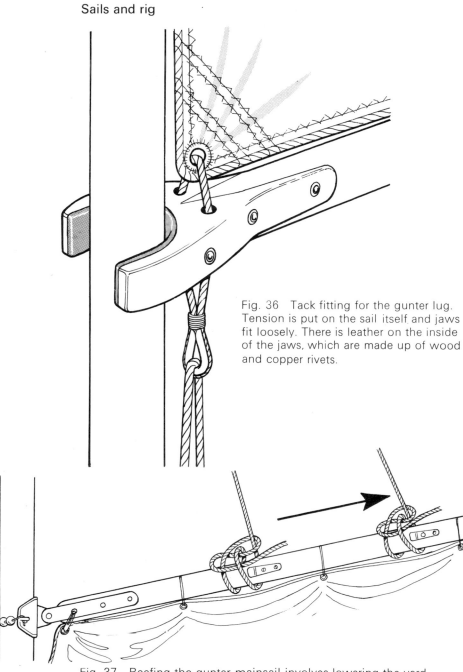

Fig. 36 Tack fitting for the gunter lug. Tension is put on the sail itself and jaws fit loosely. There is leather on the inside of the jaws, which are made up of wood and copper rivets.

Fig. 37 Reefing the gunter mainsail involves lowering the yard and changing the position of the halyard on it.

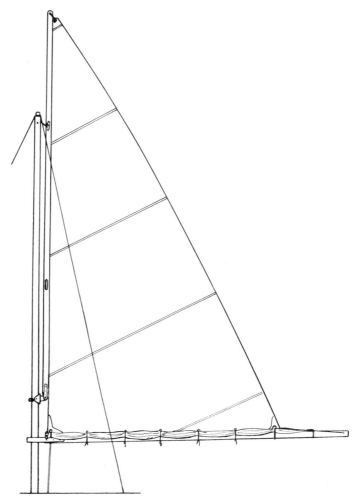

Fig. 38   The reefed gunter mainsail: in effect it has shortened the height of the mast.

be ready spliced into the eyelets, and then tying up the reef points, takes very little longer. In addition it keeps the strain on the boom end straight up and down without twist.

Another advantage of point reefing is that, if the job has been well done, it can be left when the sail is stowed, and is all ready for the sail to be used if the boat gets under way again before the weather eases.

Standing rigging for a dinghy generally consists of just three lengths of wire—two shrouds and a forestay. Nothing else is possible in a gunter-rigged boat, but a well designed and properly stepped

Bermudian mast needs nothing else either.

Lots of elderly racing dinghies are still around which have their tall masts strengthened with jumpers and spreaders, big yacht fashion. The very early Merlin Rockets were an example. Their masts were very tall—too high for a cruising dinghy, so the owner of a boat with a mast thus rigged ought to seek good advice about shortening the spar to get rid of the extra pieces of wire. Or, if this is not possible (if the mast is hollow throughout its length, for instance) fit a new, more simply rigged, mast. This should also be done if the mast has running backstays, which have to be set up on the windward side when the boat tacks, and can be quite a handful if the boat is sailed single-handed.

The Wayfarer's mast is an example of how simple the standing rigging can be on a large dinghy. She has the two shrouds and forestay, with the addition of a pair of spreaders, which move freely in their mast sockets when the strain is off the shrouds, to brace the mast against the sideways thrust of the sail.

Strength in standing rigging is just as important as simplicity, but it is worth noting that in high performance racing craft, which are

Fig. 39 Bowsprits are found on some older boats, but a major snag is that the bobstay frequently fouls the mooring.

probably more hard driven than most cruising boats, are rigged in this way. Take the Fireball dinghy for example. This has been done largely to make the mast more flexible, to give a greater control of the sail curvature for light and heavy weather, which might not concern a cruising man much. But a mast that can give a little in a puff is probably happier than one which is held rigid by unyielding triangles of wire. The important thing is to have a mast man enough for the job in cruising, so that a stouter section than that of a windage-conscious racing boat is required.

Bowsprit
Bowsprits look nice, and setting a jib out on one usually makes a boat quicker in stays, especially if she is a long, straight keeled type. But, bowsprits entail bobstays and these, if a boat is left on a mooring, spend about one per cent of their lives bowsing down the bowsprit and the other ninety nine per cent sawing through the mooring chain. (Fig. 39) Another point against bowsprits is that bending on the jib, when the boat is dancing in a loppy sea, is an arm stretching balancing act. There should be no routine work in getting a dinghy ready for sea which involves the crew getting out of the cockpit or leaning out over the bow.

Most yacht chandlers with a rigging department have a Talurit splicing machine for turning eyes in wire shrouds, but as wire splicing in the small gauges used in dinghies is easy enough to handle, many owners could while away a pleasant, if sore-thumbed winter's evening by making their own. Fig. 40 shows various ways of making an eye in the end of the rigging.

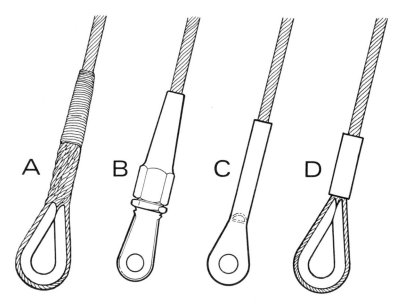

Fig. 40 Examples of available ways of fitting an eye to take lanyards. A. Back splice, which can be done at home, especially dinghy size which can be handled with small tools. B. Norseman fitting, another do-it-yourself aid: especially suitable for doing actually on mooring or beach. C. Typical swaging with a terminal. D. Talurit collar which is useful for making eye of any desired size.

**Shroud
Lanyards**

Rigging screws look neat for setting up the shrouds but shroud lanyards do the same job for a fraction of the cost. They will stand hard knocks and tugging strains that rigging screws will not tolerate.

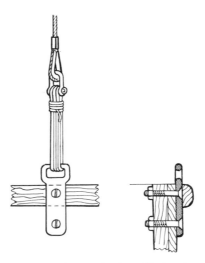

Fig. 41   Lanyards used to set up rigging. Chain plates should be bolted to hull.

(Fig. 41) They last for ages and their condition can be seen at a glance. Lanyards give warning that their time is nearly up by fraying. The fractured thread of a rigging screw gives no warning. Bend them and they will snap any time thereafter. Setting up the rigging with lanyards is a more rule-of-thumb affair, but highly tuned masts are a liability in a cruising boat. Lanyards are better able to withstand knocks against quay walls or the well-meaning tugs of helpers giving the crew a hand to get the boat on to a launching trolley. The shrouds on Frank Dye's Wayfarer, incidentally, are set up with lanyards, so they are not items suitable only for elderly knockabout boats.

The old boat rigs, standing lugsails and spritsails, beat the gunter and Bermudian hands down when it came to hoisting sail and taking it in. The standing lug, or French lug, as R. C. Leslie calls it, was probably the handiest in this respect. The yard was hoisted by a single halyard like that of a gunter lugsail, but on the standing lug the yard was held against the mast by an iron ring called a traveller. (Fig. 42) This had a hook below, and a small ring for the halyard above, set in line with each other so that the power of the hoist was transmitted through the halyard to the eye, thence to the yard via the hook.

**Lowering
Sail Quickly**

For his sixteen foot yawl-rigged open boat, Leslie recommended setting a boom at the foot of the sail to make it more manageable with the wind free, but working and Navy boats set the sail loose-footed. With its short yard set on a short mast, the standing lug could not help but come down smartly when required, and it is worth bearing in mind that to the old working boatmen, the ability to get sail in quickly in a squall was of more importance to the crew of a racing dinghy of today who, if the boat's buoyancy is as it should be, can right a capsized boat in seconds. A capsize would have been far less fun in a working boat full of fishing gear, with the crew muffled in jackets, high boots, or full-length oilskin coats and fishing aprons.

In this respect the cruising dinghy man should think more like the working boatman, and less like the racer. Of course he needs buoyancy to keep the boat afloat if she does go over. But she will be laden with camping and cooking gear, which means extra weight to get upright, and more to get damaged by being drenched or trampled on in the emergency of righting the boat. No, a capsize in a

Fig. 42   Standing lug mast traveller

cruising dinghy, which it should always be allowed for, should always be regarded as avoidable. A dinghy with the weight in the right place, with the right amount of sail set, clear of sudden blasts from high land, or large ships, and being sailed at the speed the sea conditions allow, shows a remarkable reluctance to capsize.

Letting the Main Fly

From my own experience I think that the mainsail in a well-balanced dinghy can be left aloft, but well squared off and flogging, even in quite powerful squalls. But, of course, in dinghies the crew are part of the boat. If they keep cool, shift their weight inboard and let the sheets go before the squall strikes—and the sight of one coming is unmistakable—then the boat should come to no harm.

I remember finding this out while sailing single-handed in a clinker dinghy I still own. She is gunter rigged with an area of about seventy five square feet compared with the normal racing area for a boat of her size of about ninety square feet. The breeze had gone round north west after passage of a deep depression and more settled weather was on the way, but, not without the occasional flurry of cold-front squalls. One large patch of dark cloud was converging ominously and eventually I saw the sea to windward go dark as slate with white flecks on it, and the shore disappeared in a murky veil. Just before it struck the true breeze died away. I cast off the jib sheet and pushed the idly swinging boom away to the lee side and crouched in the bottom of the boat, holding the tiller down to leeward slightly, and ready to shift my weight sharply. (Fig. 43)

There was a hiss of stinging rain and the thing was on us. Then followed the wild flogging and rattling of sails, and the flicking of jib sheets dancing like dementing snakes, which is probably more awesome in a dinghy than the weather itself. Within a few seconds the rain turned to hail, through which it was impossible to look to windward.

She lay taking it broad on the port bow. I had half raised the centreplate and she began to make a fair amount of leeway, which seemed reasonable in the circumstances and generally she seemed quite comfortable. Dead to leeward was a buoy, still a hundred yards off, but I was keen not to hit it. Inch by inch I brought the slack mainsheet in, just enough to give her a semblance of way across the wind until the buoy was safely on the quarter.

A few minutes more of the wild racket and the sky suddenly brightened, the wind ceased as if somebody had shut a door. Up to windward there was sparkling tranquility again, while the squall blotted out the horizon to leeward as it rolled ponderously on. A little time to pump the melted hail from the bottom of the boat and she was sailing again.

There was time to have got the jib in and perhaps to have lowered the main as well, and then she would have been safe as houses however much it blew. But you can only decide things like that at the time, not in an armchair. Anyway, if the sails had been off her the only way to have dealt with the problem of the buoy would have been to get the oars out and row her clear.

The point of all this is merely to underline that it is vital to get to know one's boat and how she will behave, getting experience in all the weather she can reasonably be expected to meet without foolhardy bravado and, most important, not to be too overawed by the noise, which is always one of the most daunting things about a squall because it doesn't help one to think straight.

It is worth mentioning that this dinghy has a long straight keel and skeg, and lay quietly with sail set without swerving about. It would have been more dicey in these conditions to have left the jib in a racing type with a rockered bottom, as even an empty jib could have turned her head too far off the wind causing the main to fill and press her.

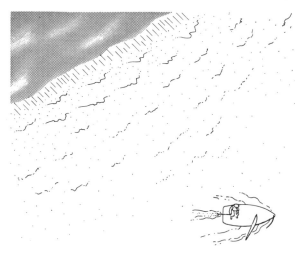

(a) Threatened by a squall: an effective technique. First watch to windward for warning of approach.

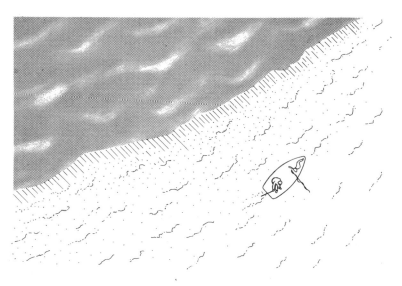

(b) Before squall strikes, point boat higher. Dowse jib, ease away mainsheet. Crew go to centre of boat, ready to shift weight quickly.

Fig. 43   Threatened by a squall in a cruising dinghy.

(c) Boat stopped and taking the wind fine on one bow, but not lying head to wind. Helm is used to keep her pointing like this.

(d) The mainsail can be hauled in gently to give some way to avoid an obstruction to leeward. The sail should not fill, just be sheeted to give minimum way.

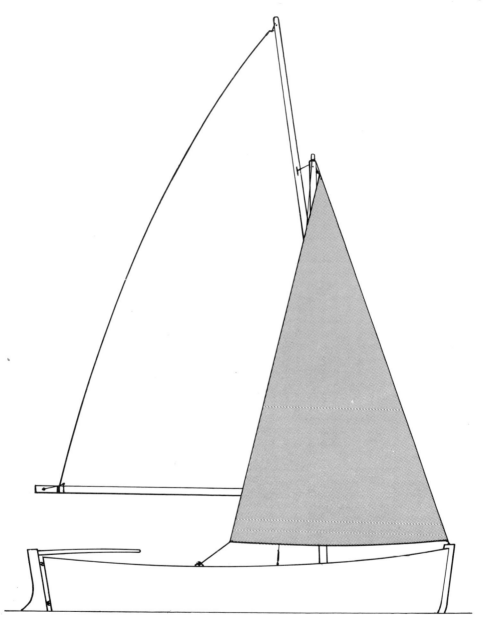

Fig. 44 For light weather a special headsail is useful. Proportions should be as shown. 1 oz terylene is a suitable weight.

Discussion of rig too often is restricted to its handiness in heavy weather, sailing in which is not most people's choice. So it is well to bear in mind that a boat's performance in light weather is just as important. At the end of a long day, when the breeze is beginning to die, the chosen haven is still a few miles to windward and there is only an hour of fair tide left, then one is glad of a boat which can go well at this time, and certainly a modern rig is favourite for these conditions.

In light weather a jib really comes into its own, although it may have been furled for most of the day for comfort. There is seldom room in a laden cruising boat to carry more than the normal working suit of sails, the clothes she stands up in you might say. But a large, light weather jib can often save an hour's rowing or shattering the peace with an outboard motor. (Fig. 44) And think how much less room an extra sail takes up than does a motor.

6 Cruising grounds

The great attraction of open boat cruising is its versatility. Rivers and inland waterways are open to a boat which can lower her mast and take an outboard motor clamped on the transom. Shallow waters and creeks and estuaries, denied to larger yachts are hers. Again, unlike her larger sisters, she is not tied to the sailing distance possible to and from her moorings in a week-end. With a car and a road trailer, and the time, the world is hers, from the Hebrides to the Greek Islands.

On a passage down the Channel coast, say, she can be left in the corner of an obliging boatyard for a few pence, and with greater peace of mind for her owner and the crew than could a yacht on the visitors' moorings in the harbour, while awaiting the crew to resume the cruise the following week-end.

This is the fascination of a good seaboat—and above everything a cruising boat must be that—which can carry her crew across miles of open water, yet be small enough in harbour to need no moorings and no tender to get ashore, just access to a smooth bit of foreshore or a public launching ramp.

One Foot on Shore

She allows more intimate exploration of a stretch of coastline than a larger craft. Except when giving the strong tides off a headland a wide berth, or making the best of a spell of good weather, to reach a desired destination, a dinghy is rarely committed to a long passage. When an attractive and safe piece of shore appears on the beam, and provided sea conditions make for a safe landing, her crew can hoist the centreplate and skim over the shallows for a closer look and a picnic on the beach.

The Solent, the rivers of Essex and Suffolk, the West Country estuaries, natural harbours like Milford Haven or that Samarkand of cruising men, the coasts and islands of Western Scotland are probably easier to reach by dinghy than by larger craft when there is a car available to tow the boat to a chosen base from which the cruise can begin.

Supposing a Solent based owner wants to explore the estuaries of South Devon and Cornwall. He can avoid the long sail down-

Channel, with the hazards like St. Aldelm's Race and the more fearsome one off Portland and start his cruise at the sailing centre of his choice, A good dinghy can cope with the Channel—so long as her owner can choose his weather. Whereas going by road may not seem good seamanship, closer study shows that this is just what it is. Seamanship means getting there safely, and not taking risks afloat because time presses.

Planning

In planning a visit like this to new waters, charts and sailing directions, while useful, give only a little of the information the dinghy man wants to know. He is less interested in the depth of the water in the deep-channel approaches to commercial harbours than in details about launching sites and dinghy parks, road access to the water and car parking. Like the yacht skipper he wants to know the names and addresses of boatyards, harbourmasters, chandleries and sailmakers, but what concerns him more is whether he can haul his boat out, and if there is a good camping site nearby, if he chooses to camp ashore.

So that a lot of the planning of a dinghy cruise in new waters means the sort of guidebook homework that shore-based holiday-makers have to do. There are excellent cruising guides now on all the popular stretches of coast in Europe that are used by yachtsmen. Less frequented shores, the very thing that makes them more attractive to dinghy sailors, are less well served. One annual publication which goes some way to fill the gap is 'Boat World' published by Sells' Publications Ltd, Epsom. This 900-page wad of useful information is one of the best buys going. It describes the main sailing centres around the coast. It lists the services available, with telephone numbers, and—just the sort of information a dinghy cruiser needs—whether visitors can use the showers and dining room in the local sailing club.

As skill, experience and a self-reliance increases, a crew can think more about planning cruises to places more off the regular cruising track. But one fact should never be forgotten. If a stretch of coast looks attractively uncrowded with boats, it's a safe bet that this is because the waters are inconvenient or unsuitable for open-boat sailing. Dinghy cruising is adventurous enough all the time, so save the pioneering stuff until you have learned all you can about a part of the coast which is attractive, about the tides, what the shore is like for landing, how the high land inshore affects the breeze, or how nearby headlands affect the tides. And always be prepared ruthlessly to scrap any sailing plans when the weather on the day gives doubt about being able to cope.

There is, of course, greater attraction in starting and finishing a cruise from one's home base, especially when one thinks of the coast roads in summer. Greatest advantage of this is that the crew will know their home waters better, and can get to know which little-used beaches make camping sites, or the handy anchorages close inshore where only a few tiny craft can venture.

7 Dinghy camping

Open-boat cruising is really the art of making do. You make do with a small boat for a start. And if you don't think that has its attractions you will probably not have read this far. You make do with a few simple essentials instead of the mass of gear which the well-equipped cruising yacht carries. Not because it is unnecessary, but simply because there is not room for it.

A yacht has her bilge pump and toilet. A dinghy has a plastic bucket which serves for both purposes. A yacht has a galley of sorts in which food can be prepared under way in fair weather. In a dinghy, good sailing weather means that everything else but sailing is difficult or impossible. So the wise crew fills vacuum flasks with soup or coffee before starting, and keeps biscuits handy in a waterproof jar to munch on passage.

One thing which no cruising dinghy, however small, can do without is comfortable sleeping arrangements for the number who will normally sail in her. There are two schools of thought about the advantage of sleeping aboard, with the extra independence and privacy this offers, or of camping ashore, where there is more space to stretch and elbow room for the cook. Good camping sites along the foreshore are often hard to find, and a weary crew may have to dabble through thick mud to get to them, leaving the boat at anchor until she can be floated in on the tide. The simple answer is to have versatile gear which makes both courses of action possible as required, although this brings us back to the problem of how much gear to carry. There is no shame in roughing it in comfort and a good night's sleep in the warm and dry should be regarded as the most important part of the cruise routine—even more important than food, which can, if need be, come from shops and cafés.

Limited Space

The limitation of stowage space which a dinghy imposes means that the crew has to be small in number. Two is about ideal. A dinghy of suitable size for parents to handle can cope with a family of children as well for day-sailing. But unless their warmth and comfort can be assured when a cruise extends overnight, it would be advisable to plan in terms of a small decked yacht with bunks. At the same time it is well to rid dinghy cruising of its image as a tough, dare-devil sport for impecunious young men who happily spend hours driving to windward on the open sea, and who sleep serenely on an exposed beach at the end of the day.

There are such people, and we can be grateful to them as the Slocums and McMullens of our day, who have shown what open centre-board boats are capable of when handled well. But for most owners a leisurely cruise to a peaceful creek a few miles away at which to spend the night is the ideal combination of adventure and relaxation. If a cruising dinghy is worthy of the name, she must have some sleeping space inside for the crew, plus room to set up a small stove to prepare simple hot food. A cruise can be spoilt if there is too much dependance on the amenities ashore, and pleasant camping sites near the water do not always have a gently sloping beach on which to run the boat ashore. Anchorage suitable for small centre-board boats, on the other hand, are easy to find even in the most crowded yachting centres. Take the most crowded of them all, the Hamble River, for example.

Down each side of the main channel during the season lies an unbroken line of moored yachts, all the way from Bursledon Bridge to the mouth. Inshore of the moorings, there are many stretches of this still delightful river where a dinghy can lie, and take the ground on the mud, out of the way of the big traffic and with the prospect of pleasant hinterland.

Deep water sailors often smile at the advice to dinghy cruisers to pack a countryside map as well as a chart. Well, still with the Hamble River as an example let the dinghy skipper study the map showing the remaining tidal part of the river upstream from Bursledon Bridge to Botley and he will find between the two a stretch of unspoiled river awaiting his exploration, the only price of admission being the need to lower his mast to get under the road bridge. The map will show him lanes and footpaths from the shore to the village and the shops. I know many yachtsmen who know harbours in plenty on the other side of the Channel, but who are unaware of the beauties which exist on their own home waters. Adventurous dinghy owners should not be so remiss.

Sleeping Aboard

The main requirement for turning an open boat into sleeping quarters is a tent cover. (Fig. 45) Simple enough to make, using the boom, which is shipped into a crutch at the aft end, as the ridgepole, the cover is then lashed to the mast at the forward end, and made fast along the sides with eyelets which fit into lacehooks outside the gunwale. (Fig. 46) The cover should be made high-sided enough to allow the boom to be triced up a couple of feet before rigging the tent cover to allow stooping room inside.

The success of a cruise can stand or fall by how comfortable the crew can be at the end of the day. The camping tent cover for setting up in the boat itself will almost certainly have to be a one-off job, designed for the boat. Efforts by manufacturers of boats like the Wayfarer and Mirror 16 dinghies to offer standard covers have not been successful as owners appear to prefer to make their own.

Planning a   When planning the cover, you must decide how much headroom
Tent Cover   can be allowed by setting the boom and gaff as high as possible in
the crutch, how the lacings are to be fastened to the outside of the
hull, and where the lacehooks are to be fitted. Abaft the mast,
getting the measurements is simple enough. Just take the distance
from the top of the stowed boom or gaff down to the gunwale at
parallel six-inch intervals, then allow extra length for a shallow skirt
outside the hull. What needs special care—but not special skill— is

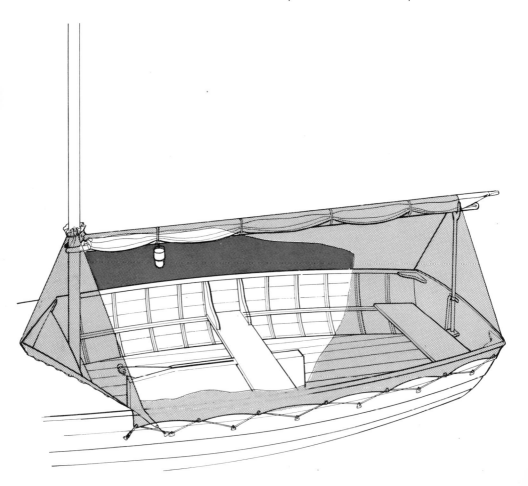

Fig. 45 The basis for camping is a tent cover. The main boom is
used as a ridge pole. A light can be hung from this : a battery lantern
is advisable.

getting the measurements right for the part which goes forward of the mast and has to tuck snugly around the bows, or under the washboards.

Sailmakers are nearly always most helpful men, and will advise on what measurements to take. Alternatively stout brown paper can be used to make a pattern. One vital point; design everything in terms of the tent cover having to be erected from inside the boat. Remember that when anchored in deep water, there is no chance of stepping outside to get at an awkwardly placed lacing. Another hint is to

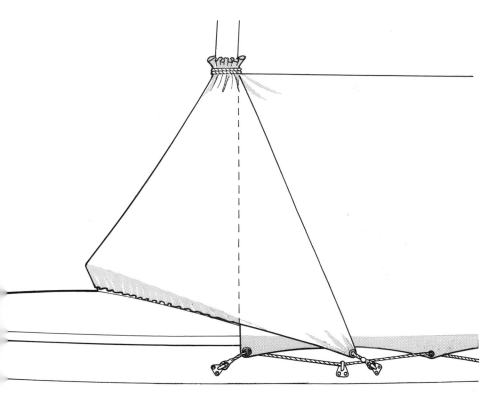

Fig. 46   How to deal with the forward end of the tent. A foredeck is essential for this arrangement. The tent is cut to overlap the breakwater and wrap back round to the side of the tent.

make the cover so that it can be rolled forward and tied with reef points midway along its length, so that in fine weather, the after part of the boat can be left open.

Foredecks, preferably with generous washboards, prove their worth in fitting a cover, as the fore end of it can be tailored to fit over the washboards, where they can be held securely against a gale by a simple elastic drawstring. I advocate this instead of a more

Close-fitting floorboards make a more comfortable sleeping platform than the open type. The toe-straps on the centreboard case are mounted high to allow room for sleeping.

elaborate lacing so that the skipper can open up the fore end quickly and tend to the anchor warp if need be.

As for the aft end, this should be left open. Two people asleep in a small boat, need at least this much ventilation. The boat will lie head to wind and in several seasons of sleeping aboard my boat I was never attacked from the rear by the weather. Sleeping bags are so good and so cheap these days that their place aboard is taken for granted. Two basic rules are to buy a bag with the heaviest available weight of filling, and to make sure that it has a nylon zip fastener or one of alloy which will not corrode and jam in salt air. The best range of sleeping bags is that of Blacks of Greenock Ltd., Industrial Estate, Port Glasgow, Renfrewshire, Scotland. They make bags for polar explorers and Everest climbers as well as campers and dinghy cruisers and their illustrated catalogue—it includes tents as well— is worth study. Remember that a waterproof groundsheet is necessary if there is any risk of bilge water touching the bag from under the bottom boards.

When at anchor, the spars should be kept up clear of the boat, to provide more room, and to make the ridge pole for the tent. The fore-end of the spars can be held in place to the mast either by the gooseneck or by taking a turn with the slack halyard to set them at the required height. (Fig. 47)

Boom Crutch   At the after end, a boom crutch is necessary. Do not use the scissors type, which is an abomination, and will collapse if any weight is put on it. Instead, fashion a slotted anchoring point for fastening either to the stern athwart, or the transom for a single pillar type crutch, shaped like the handle of a garden spade, without the crossbar at the top which the digger grips.

Sleeping bags keep out the cold, but not the wet, and bottom boards of most dinghies are too near the hull planking to protect a sleeper from any but the slightest trace of bilge water. (Fig. 48) Exceptions are the Wayfarer and the Drascombe boats which have the bottom boards, raised well clear of the hull bottom. In less well-endowed boats an air bed can be used as a damp barrier, but this often raises the sleeper so close to the thwarts that he cannot

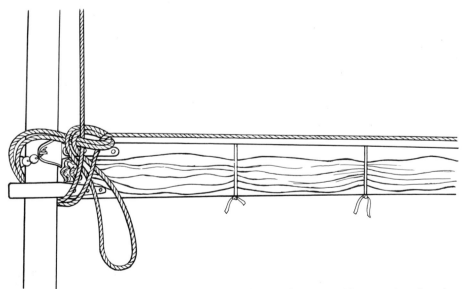

Fig. 47   For gunter rig, mainsail must be stowed between yard and boom. The halyard can be used to lash both spars at desired height when camping.

turn in his sleep. In this case a waterproof groundsheet will not only serve as efficiently, but will also be easier to prepare and stow away. A pillow might be considered a luxury until you have tried sleeping without one. Rolled up sweaters are just not the same. I always take a proper pillow, in its own polythene bag. It does more for a good night's sleep afloat than anything else.

Cooking   For cooking I found that the safest and simplest appliance is the paraffin pressure stove, of which the Primus is the best-known example. Bottled gas is fine for the galley of a yacht which has a

The author's 12-footer, preparing for sea. In a boat of this size the absence of decking gives more room to work.

built-in stove, but the tiny versions sold in camping shops seem to lack the robust simplicity of the Primus. Paraffin can be carried in a plastic container, and with this fuel one can always see at a glance how much is left—not always so with gas bottles. Methylated spirits for priming should not be carried in an ordinary bottle, which tends to slop too much into the ignition pan, but in an oil can with a nozzle which will direct just the right amount into the pan without spilling.

For carrying the stove when not in use, I made a box of marine ply

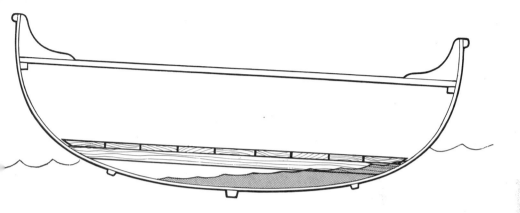

Fig. 48 Raised bottom boards keep small amount of bilge water clear when camping, but most dinghies have negligible space below bottom boards.

off cuts, with a skirted lift-off lid without hinges which proved completely waterproof. Remember that matches need to be packed as carefully as dry clothes. A good plan is to store boxes along with other gear that must be kept dry, like spare torch batteries, and tobacco, in a screw-top kitchen jar which can be bought from most ironmongers.

Dry Locker   For general dry stowage, and as a food locker, I recommend a version of the old sea chest, which can be made at home. (Fig. 49) Mine was, like the Primus box, made of marine ply and fitted on the bowsheets under the foredeck. It had lifting handles, and carried almost as easily as a canvas holdall.

To make it as waterproof as possible, I suggest that the lid be of the lift-off type with a deep skirt all round. Even the best amateur carpenter would be hard put to make a simple hinged lid proof against the direct hit of a dollop of spray, which is the regular lot of all gear in a dinghy. Plastic bags are fine, but they should not be used without an outer, tougher wrapping, or the first slightest snag of a sharp projection will ruin them. A good arrangement for each member of the crew is a canvas kit-bag, which will hold his sleeping bag and dry clothes, each of which has its own inner polythene bag

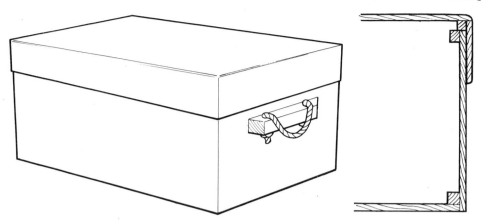

Fig. 49   Plywood stowage box is light weight and can be made to fit the particular dinghy. Lid with deep skirt keeps out water.

lining. Any good sailing breeze, even on a fine summer's day, will send spray flying over the weather bow into a dinghy, so good stowage is vital all the time. An efficient all-round light, which can stand on a thwart, or hang from the boom-cum-ridgepole, should be carried. (Fig. 45) The best I know is the battery-operated Tildawn, which has a protected dome, like that on a motor mechanic's inspection lamp, mounted on a hard rubber base, which holds the batteries.

The beauty of the Tildawn is that it can be carried hung dome-downwards, where it is out of the way and sheds the most efficient light throughout the boat. Avoid flame lights, not only because of their obvious danger if knocked over, but because their fumes are not healthy in such a confined space. The Tildawn might seem too rugged a job, but the only alternatives seem to be flimsy oriental imports which give up the ghost at the slightest knock. Nothing can be too rugged for a dinghy cruising.

8 Clothes for Cruising

Making a Choice

Any old clothes will do for sailing on a fine day, but for cruising a little more thought is needed. In an open boat there is no shelter for the crew other than the clothes they wear, and these need to be efficient and comfortable. With so much good sailing gear in the shops these days, the problem is to make a choice. The market is competitive, and standards are usually high. The buyer gets what he pays for, and lightweight smocks and trousers might seem a bargain when their low price is compared, but they are not so tough or reliable. Nothing is more miserable or useless in a boat than oilskins that leak.

Kitting out for cruising is based on the obvious principle of a thick layer of absorbent, air-trapping garments, inside an impermeable top layer of oilies. Skins are designed to keep you dry rather than warm, and woollen sweaters are not much good exposed to wind and spray. Woollen vests with short sleeves are a good buy for sailing. These can be bought from Government surplus stores, or from clothiers who specialize in catering for workmen engaged in tough jobs. A year or two ago the editor of a yachting magazine launched a welcome campaign to bring back shirts with long tails. One maker advertises these. Ordinary shirts, which ride out of trouser tops, are not good, because a dinghy man spends most of his sailing time either stooping or sitting hunched up. Thick woollen working shirts are best. They are warmer, and they can be worn for several days before they begin to look too obviously grubby. And that means that you don't have to pack so many.

Boots—not Shoes

Canvas topped shoes are good only for a short sail on a warm day. They are miserable to wear when wet, which means nearly all the time in a dinghy. At night, when a cold dew always seems to settle on the sea, they are torture. Much more practical is a pair of short sailing boots, worn over a single pair of woollen socks. Do not be tempted to wear two pairs of socks. This will make the boots a tight fit, and squeeze out the air insulation. Boots store heat well, and when a cupful of spray finds its way in under the oilskin trouser bottoms, it soon warms up.

Cold draughts are the biggest enemy. On a wet skin a mild summer breeze can feel like a mid-winter nor-easter after only a few minutes—a situation which can lead to serious danger of exposure, if it goes on too long over a large area. Even wet clothes can help to keep the body heat in if oilskins are worn to keep out the cold wind, and any wind is a cold wind when the body is wet. Warmth means more than comfort. It means no fatigue or that dangerous mental lethargy which comes when one has been exposed to the cold for only a short time. Pressure on packing space means that dinghy cruisers usually sleep in their day clothes. Washing tends to get neglected or postponed until a hospitable club is reached which makes its showers available to visitors.

Going Ashore   Much of the fun of cruising is a visit ashore, to go shopping or to see the sights. Nobody will be relaxed if he has to walk around in soggy sailing shoes, shorts or oilies, so it is worth while finding room for proper walking shoes and a pair of less shabby trousers. If you plan to visit sailing clubs to do a bit of socializing, it is still considered good manners, even in these less stuffy days, to wear a tie, and a clean pair of socks, especially if you get an invitation to dinner. You may not be that well in socially, but shore clothes are always more comfortable ashore, just as sailing clothes are afloat.

A useful piece of sailing wear, too often neglected except by people who know about sailing in poor weather, is a towel scarf, or roll-mop. This can make a world of difference to comfort, both in keeping the warm air from escaping around the collar, and for keeping the spray out. If you wear a hat, make sure it will stay on. A woollen bonnet, like the other gear, helps to trap the warmth and is useful when worn inside the foul-weather hoods fitted to so many oilskin jackets. It prevents the tendency to stay put when you turn your head, which can cut off your vision in a most disconcerting way. A hood is welcome in really miserable weather, but if one is worn it should have efficient buttoning under the chin to make sure it fits snugly against the cheeks and turns when the head turns.

Gloves? Yes, by all means. Many a hardened ocean racing man is glad of a pair of mittens to slip on at night, or when the weather is chilly. I have known sea passages where a pair of woollen gloves has been ceremoniously exchanged between the helmsman and his relief at the change of watch. Why gloves should be thought cissy and woolly hats not, I fail to understand. Surely a pair of hands are more useful when the fingers are not numb with the cold. Like socks gloves are better than bare skin even when they are wet. A favourite all-weather garment for any small-boat sailor is the canvas smock. This gives windproof protection when the weather is too light to justify oilskins. Most people wear oilskin trousers all the time, even when the top is not worn, so trousers should be chosen for their ability to absorb condensation. Flannel or corduroy are favourites.

Polar Suit   Years ago the United States Army announced a research campaign to find a utility garment which could be worn in all climates, and at all times of the day. I wonder what became of the idea. The nearest thing the small-boat sailor has to this ideal so far is the polar suit type, like a close fitting track suit, faced with a thick pile on the inside and with a fabric weave on the outside. This would seem to be the perfect answer for sailors. Draughtproof, highly efficient for heat storage, and with the ability to absorb perspiration away from the skin (important when one is encased in oilskins for a long time) and quick drying. One polar suit could probably do the work of all the other sweaters, trousers and vests which take up so much room in the crewman's kitbag.

As for foul weather clothing, which we still call oilskins, although they are P.V.C., because everybody knows what the word means, there are types galore, from rugged dreadnoughts, that almost stand up by themselves, to delicate see-through creations like pocket raincoats. Oilskins are so important that it is better to study as many manufacturers' leaflets as possible before making a choice. In this way you are better prepared for the bewildering array which greets you in the clothing department of a yacht chandlers these days. One-piece, boiler-suit types are fine, but remember you have to wear the whole thing all the time. On many days the top part can be best left off for an airing.

High Waist Trousers

Never buy the ordinary waist high oilskin trousers for serious sailing. Go instead for the high fitting type, the tops of which will come up nearly to your armpits. One spends most dinghy time bent double. Trousers of conventional height would ride down in this attitude, leaving the back exposed, while the high-fitting type gives the wearer the much-needed extra freeboard. Ensure that the trousers are supported by a stout pair of braces, and that they are not too tight fitting. If they are, they will restrict both movement and air insulation. If possible, choose a smock with pockets, or with a kangaroo pouch on the chest. And make sure you transfer to them all the things likely to be needed, like handkerchief, cigarette lighter, pocket knife or shackle key. It saves a dreadful rummage later on.

9 Some racing

Racing and cruising people generally go their own ways, but there is a trend gaining a lot of support, for cruising folk to hold races on their own. With none of the needle sharpness of the real rule-book stuff, but sometimes more to their taste : a week-end amble to a popular anchorage and back, enlivened by some competition on the outward passage, a social evening at a waterside pub before the return sail next day.

Cruising men like company. What they don't much care for is having to be too much like other people. Therefore the cruiser race, provided it is not organized to death, and provided the *ad hoc* handicapping system does not involve too much work or too many sums, is a good way of brushing up sailing skill and seeing some interesting country at the same time. Dinghies were involved in such races some time before the family cruising yachts caught on. Most small clubs have for years organized something of the kind at least once a season. Clubs on the mainland side of the Solent, for example, arrange passage races to the Isle of Wight, to the Newtown River, or to the Folly Inn (beloved of week-enders) on the River Medina upstream from Cowes.

Passage Racing

Look down the sailing fixtures of any club in the area and you will find 'Passage Race to Folly' scheduled at least once. These outings usually manage to attract owners who never race in the conventional eternal-triangle way. Cruising dinghies are especially welcome and the owners of a roomy boat will, some days before the event, find themselves suddenly extra popular with racing dinghy owners, seeking stowage space for sleeping bags for which their own boats have no room.

Passage races, then, are regulars in the fixture lists. Much more rare, sadly, are the long-distance races which involve two or more full days' sailing, with less attention paid to the social life ashore in the evening, but involving camping ashore, or sleeping aboard at the turn-point, or at stages along the way.

Coronation Year, 1953, and a few seasons thereafter, was a great time for daring dinghy men keen on racing further afield. The Cowes

Corinthian Club's round-the-island dinghy race was followed a few
years later by an even more ambitious Channel crossing. These
were races proper, not cruises in company, and in the round-the-
island, several new designs from men like Uffa Fox and Ian Proctor
made their debut, and sailed along with veterans for miles around.
Sad to think that such races became less and less practicable as
the years went by. For one thing, racing and cruising men seem to
have drawn even further apart, with the increasing commercial
pressures on the former. Another reason which makes would-be
organizers think twice, is that, with the growth of boat owners, just

Cockpit of the Drascombe Lugger which David Pyle sailed from
Emsworth to Australia. The raised foredeck and extra stowage
lockers abaft the mast were owner's modifications.

one mention of such a race would bring in applicants by the mailbag full, quite a lot of them from relative newcomers to open-sea sailing whose enthusiasm would probably exceed their experience. So a maximum number of competitors has to be set, and these are chosen only if they pass a competence check.

Safety Measures

Safety precautions have reached such a sophisticated level these days, that no club would feel it was doing right by its competitors without a fleet of safety launches, all with their two way radios. Sometimes the Services are willing to help, for they find that such races are useful as communications training for their personnel. Without such help the chance of mustering a suitable number of properly equipped safety launches (it's considered bad form to call them rescue launches) would be virtually impossible. A club which has tackled the problem twice with conspicuous success is that at Lee-on-Solent, Hampshire, which in 1965, and 1967 organized a two-day passage race from Lee (midway between the Hamble River entrance and Portsmouth) to Poole and back of 30 miles, with a compulsory stop each way at Hurst, at the western end of the Solent. To be sure these were true races, with starting lines, handicap divisions and competition, but as a day long sail, over waters new to many competitors, the race could not help becoming slightly more relaxed and friendly than the usual inshore event. Lee-on-Solent Sailing Club provided an extra service which few dinghy cruisers could lay on for themselves—a shuttle lorry service which took sleeping bags and shore-going clothes on ahead to await owners at the finish. The classes which sailed in those two races are another reminder of the vague division between racing and cruising types. Cherubs, Graduates, Fireballs, Hornets and Flying Dutchmen settled down to the long haul along with the more conventional cruising types, the Yachting World Dayboats, Solent Seagulls, Wayfarers and the Salcombe Yawl, which added a graceful touch with its two masts to the 1967 race.

Early in 1972 there was talk of what promised to be the most interesting of these racing-cum-cruising meetings—one from Portsmouth to Plymouth and back, with compulsory overnight stops along the way. The idea for this originally came from David Pyle of Emsworth, Hampshire, who three years ago sailed a Drascombe Lugger with one shipmate to Australia, most of the way on open sea, with some short-cut stretches inland, such as the passage of the French canals and down the River Tigris to the Indian Ocean. Pyle conceived the voyage as a demonstration to young people that real cruising is not the preserve of big boats and big crews, (and big expenses). A small, relatively cheap open boat could, he felt, give an owner all he wanted in the way of real sailing at a reasonable cash outlay.

The original down-channel race was certainly ambitious—Pyle's suggested course was from Langstone Harbour, to the Wolf Rock, and thence back to Penzance. Controlling a racing fleet of dinghies in the precarious conditions at the mouth of the Channel would have been a superhuman job for anybody, so it was no surprise when the suggested course was eventually shortened to Plymouth. Langstone Sailing Club, which originally planned to undertake the organization of the race, had to withdraw because of the urgent need to safeguard the club's future in the face of proposed road works in their area. By the spring of 1972 there was talk of firm interest by commercial sponsors, and the race organization had been taken on by Eastney Cruising Association, which is based at the mouth of Langstone Harbour. But progress reports were few and shortly afterwards it was announced that the race had been postponed to another year. Talk of commercial sponsorship is a touchy subject, and one comes a long way from the original conception of dinghy cruising as the simplest and cheapest way of sailing in races of this sort. The average owner would find difficulty in finding time to take part.

Things seem to become less matey when there is something to be won. Perhaps it is better for the cruiser, when he feels like an occasional race for a lark, to settle for the 'Passage Race to Folly'. That's fun enough. As for the more ambitious voyage down-Channel, it is more satisfying done in one's own time, and with a handful of companions of one's own choosing, with, perhaps, more sense of achievement at the end.

10 Companions

There is no freedom to match sailing alone. A single-hander is his own master in the perfect sense. He makes all the decisions, does not have to explain to anybody his reasons for them, nor for changing his mind. It is surprising how this adds immensely to self-confidence. Sailing a boat. usually means plenty to do all the time, so there is seldom time to feel lonely, unless the weather starts to look grim, then a bit of companionship can be a boost. Choosing a dinghy for single-handed sailing needs slightly more care than a larger yacht, which does not need the crew's weight in the right place all the time to keep her upright. But in a boat which is not too heavy or lively for one, the handling of gear is simple enough.

Some items need special attention. Cam cleats on the jib sheet leads are necessary, when there is no crew to hold on to them, a downhaul on the jib, so that it can be brought into the boat quickly with one hand, and the halyard led aft within reach of the helmsman, so that he can cast if off without having to leave the helm are examples.

A crew is important when longer voyages are attempted. The time factor alone makes them too much for one, and a crew is needed to take a turn at the helm so that the skipper can get some rest. Taking watches in turns, with the man off watch sleeping on the weather side of the boat, means that two men can stay reasonably alert for long periods, whereas one would be exhausted.

Sharing the Load

More than two people in a dinghy is a crowd. But there is no need to be committed to two. The simple answer is to use more than one boat, and organize a cruise in company. This is useful when one boat, cramped for space, can beg a lift for some bulky gear in the other. Pleasures are usually the better shared, especially in the company of family or like-minded friends. Much as I love sailing alone, I like better the company when the squadron of boats reunites at a pre-arranged destination at the end of the day, when many hands can make light work of jobs like food preparation, beaching boats and pitching tents, or running errands to the shops.

The moral support of other boats within sight—and cruising

company does not mean being stuck in tight formation all day long—
is welcome when tackling a stretch of strange coast, when the
daylight begins to fail, and when the destination seems reluctant to
get closer. The secret of success is to avoid making plans which are
too detailed or too rigid. To agree on a meeting place at the end
of the day is usually enough, and this allows individual boats either
to explore inshore, or to take a straight course between headlands as
the crews think fit. In this way, if suitable boats are available, crews
and gear can be apportioned so that each boat has enough and no
more. With more stowage space available, the gear does not have to
be quite so spartan. Cruises in company like this should be planned
to avoid over-optimistic estimates of distance. To make an easy
passage between two points is far more fun and far more practicable
than trying to over-stretch everybody by aiming too far.

One thing I have never been able to explain is that a group of
people eat far more individually than a man on his own. So allow
for this when you get together to draw up the provisions before the
start.

11 Pathfinders

Dinghy cruising has a longer history than many people realize, as a direct heir to the ancient art of open-boat sailing on the sea. Yachts with lids on are new-fangled by comparison, unless you count Noah's Ark. The most interesting sailing yarns are those in which the reader can reasonably imagine himself taking part. Following Chichester or Rose round the Horn is one thing, admiration or awe. Accompanying E. F. Knight on his voyage in a converted ship's lifeboat to the Baltic, or John Seymour on the same waters in his coble, Willynilly, entirely open except for a not very efficient tent cover, is something different. Any small boat sailor with a taste for similar voyages can imagine himself with such men. High adventure is fine for heroes. For most people, low adventure is good enough. When such adventure is concerned with unremarkable boats which are available to all, and when they are concerned with a few week's holiday cruising instead of a two-year circumnavigation, then the reader becomes part of the enterprise and not just a spectator.

Marvellous voyages have been made in dinghies by men like Frank Dye, who sailed a Wayfarer across the North Sea to Norway and Denmark and across the North Atlantic to Iceland, and by Peter Clutterbuck, another Wayfarer man, who has cruised across the Channel to the Islands, thence to Britanny, round the corner past Ushant, and down the Bay of Biscay to the Midi Canal and into the Mediterranean.

These voyages may have a touch of St. Brendan fantasy about them, but they are made more often than people think. People like Dye and Clutterbuck write well about them and they get known. Others don't bother to put pen to paper and their voyages are remembered by word of mouth only. I remember being at Cherbourg one day and watching a Wayfarer glide in, almost becalmed in the narrow entrance, with a French courtesy flag and a Q flag adorning her shrouds. She returned home safely. This was about the time, I remember, when two young chaps crossed from the Channel Islands to visit relatives on the mainland, a distance of ninety miles and with exceptionally strong tides to be overcome. They did the journey both ways in a rowing boat.

The 16 ft. Wayfarer has proved a very capable cruising dinghy.
Dimensions are LWL 14 ft. 10 in., beam 6 ft. 1 in., draft 8 in. and
with plate down 3 ft. 10 in. She weighs 365 lb.

Channel Crossings

Channel crossings, the long ones I mean, from Cherbourg to the Wight, have been made several times. Journeys of this magnitude are never without their moments of gnawing anxiety, sleeplessness and the conviction that such self-inflicted suffering must be the ultimate madness. Such long sails are not everybody's cup of tea, then neither is dinghy cruising at all. But there is no harm in being reminded that small open boats can go to sea, if well handled, and keep their crews safe if, perhaps, not comfortable.

Sailing abounds in characters, individual people who go their own way in their own sort of craft. The only fault of racing is that it discourages just this. One of my favourites is an elderly gentleman, Talbot Kirk, who virtually lives aboard a thirteen foot Sharpie called Pat, which is based at Helston in Cornwall. His idea of a Channel crossing is to tackle the widest and most perilous part, from Cornwall to Britanny. In 1972 he was planning a more extended voyage, harbour hopping down the Breton coast and back, by way of the Brest-Nantes Canal, to St. Malo and home to the Helford river.

'From St. Malo we home on the Roches Douvres radio beacon and then hope to pick up the St. Mawgan beacon in Cornwall,' he wrote in the Dinghy Cruising Association Bulletin when inviting applications for a crew. 'Unfortunately there is a low power beacon at nearby St. Brieuc which is almost bang on top of St. Mawgan on the dial. But anyway with the Scillies and Ushant beacons, and the Consol station in Britanny, and the compass, navigation should not be too difficult.' Remember, it's a thirteen foot dinghy he is writing about.

Go Quietly

A thing to avoid on cruises much more modest than any of these, is the ceremonial send-off. The day you tell everyone that you are off (if you care for publicity that much) is the day it blows half a gale. In dinghy cruising one must always be prepared to cancel plans at the last minute, depending on the weather, and the crew must always feel completely free to go or stay. Even a group of well meaning friends mustered at the launching site on the big day to see them off can put unwarranted pressure on a crew to go, when the seamanlike thing would be to stay a day. Incidentally, while on the safety tack, it is amazing how meagre is the knowledge of parents, or wives about one's boat if they have occasion to make inquiries about her down the coast.

Letting People Know

Coastguards and harbourmasters are stumped unless they can be given the length and type of construction, type of rig, and colour of sails, the hull colour, how many crew are aboard, and what colour sailing clothes they are likely to be wearing. Folks back home *do* worry if time goes by without a word, and since it is now standard practice for skippers of fully crewed ocean racers to be instructed to telephone if they have been delayed, or have made an unscheduled stop 'to allay any anxiety of relatives without delay' then all the more reason for the crew of an open boat to do so.

The sea is a lonely and uncomfortable place, and I confess my taste in cruising yarns is for something more homely than ocean passages. There is more useful stuff to learn. Give me the day's run along a coast or between islands, with a stop ashore at evening, and leave the vast wastes of open water to ocean cruising men, who can retire to their bunks and listen to the rain drumming on deck during their watch below. One such tale is that of a ten foot dinghy called Curlew, which two members of Portsmouth Sailing Club, S. Searl, and P. Glover, sailed up-channel to Dover and back in 1930, when dinghy cruising was even less fashionable than it is now.

Voyages

They carried their keep-drys in a wooden box with a padlock, lashed abaft the centre thwart, standing on a lifebelt, with a waterproof groundsheet entirely covering it. A hurricane lamp was kept lashed to a shroud and the water was stowed in a tin can bought from the ironmongers because 'the usual stone jar which most sailing men carry for the stowage of water was voted too heavy for our purpose.' Gear has progressed since then. !

The pair took to the oars when the wind fell away, and hauled the boat up the beach at a convenient stopping place. In those days there must have been more disused cottages and buildings near the seashore for a night's sleep in the dry. Otherwise, if the weather was fine, they slept in the open, which must have been a poor second best. Towards the end of their week-long cruise the weather began to break up. They spent a night at Folkstone and at six the next morning launched into a sea left by a thunder storm during the night. 'There was a light wind from the north-west and on the last of the ebb we made good way across the tide towards Cap Griz Nez, our hoped-for destination.' When the wind died they rowed, with the shipping in the Strait causing them 'anxiety'. When the breeze freshened they tucked in two reefs in the gunter mainsail and ran back for Dover. Time was short, so they sent Curlew home by rail, and walked the whole way themselves.

In a twelve foot dinghy called Stormalong, similarly gunter rigged, two brothers, Christopher and Sandy Paine, voyaged from Corran in Loch Linnhe, round the south west of Mull to Iona, then across the open Atlantic to Tyree, thence to the neighbouring island of Coll to the north, and back home along the north coast of Mull, rejoining Loch Linnhe by way of the Sound of Mull. The Western Isles have a special evocative fascination for boat sailors, but their strong tides and weather, which is more rugged than that of the South, are not for novices. The Paine brothers cruised in a twelve footer, and slept in tents ashore. The small boat was of ideal size for beaching and launching by two, and the shortage of space for stowage was probably well worth putting up with for that.

**Problems
with a
Heavy Boat**

This was borne out by John Weaver and his wife Susan whose cruise in a Wayfarer around Mull in 1963, over some of the waters cruised by the Paines, earned for them the Frank Dye Cruising Trophy for that year.

'Mooring proved to be a problem throughout the cruise,' John

Launching and recovery of heavy dinghies is made easier with a combination trolley-trailer. This example, available from J. L. Gmach & Co. Ltd., of Fordingbridge, Hampshire, comprises a light launching trolley which rides with the boat on the road trailer. The trailer is thus spared immersion in salt water.

Weaver wrote. 'There was a choice of bringing the boat ashore, and risking damage on rocks overnight, or anchoring her in deeper water and having to wait until low tide to get aboard.' Nothing is perfect, and the Weavers' Wayfarer, a better boat for the open sea than Stormalong or Curlew, was heavier to handle ashore. You take your choice : a small boat for handiness and lightness, which can be brought ashore on a pocket handkerchief of smooth beach, or a larger, heavier boat, fine for open sea passages, but needing more care in choosing hauling-out spots.

A. G. Earl, another pioneer dinghy cruiser, used a ten-footer rigged with a gunter lugsail without jib, for cruises up and down the Channel coast single-handed—and slept aboard what's more. So really it all comes back to the crew every time. A well built and sensibly rigged boat ten feet long, can go as far as a longer dinghy : the difference is that it will take longer both because of actual boat speed and the likelihood of remaining in port because of unsuitable conditions.

12 Lay up and plan again

The season advances. All too soon there is a nip in the air and darkness comes earlier. Cruising days are nearly over for another year. But with a dinghy there are still plenty of chances to go sailing on those occasional fine and mellow days which faithfully brighten up the English winter. This is another advantage of a boat small enough to live ashore between sails. She is protected from the bad weather, and is always ready for action in the good. Working on a boat ashore is easier than on a craft lying afloat and this means that with the splendidly efficient paint and finishes today, a one hour spell of touching up occasionally during the summer keeps the boat fit to stay in commission for winter sailing.

The best piece of gear for keeping her in good order is a weatherproof cover, fitted with deep skirts around the sides and preferably made of heaviest, toughest material available. The cost of a good cover is high in proportion to the costs of running a dinghy, but a good one will last several years, and preserve the inside of the boat from the weather, and thereby cut drastically the amount of repainting or revarnishing required. A heavy flax canvas cover is as good as any, and can be reproofed easily. It is extremely difficult to damage, and although waterproof will allow enough air through the weave to prevent condensation, which is what makes plastic covers unacceptable in a wooden boat.

Security
A cover also provides security. A small dinghy, because of the job she does, is bound to be more cluttered with gear than a racing craft, much of which can conveniently stay aboard, hidden under the cover. This ability to keep the gear from prying eyes is particularly valuable when she is left unattended, or is left unattended at a harbour down the coast between one weekend sail and the next.

The enforced idleness of winter allows time for looking back on the cruises of the season gone and using them to plan ventures in the warmer months to come. It is a time for converting the battered, salt-stained and dog-eared passage log into something more lasting and informative. Photographs can enliven a good log, and while the chances for taking pictures are limited in a dinghy under way (cameras have a hard life in open boats) there is always a chance for that most fascinating of all pictures when cruising—the view of a new harbour or unvisited anchorage framed between the foredeck and the foot of the jib of one's own boat.

Cruise Log Competitions

Another old pictorial favourite is one's own boat at anchor, framed in a bay or cove. A cruise log, rewritten as a narrative, can be made into an entry for the log competitions which many sailing clubs hold.

For one's own benefit, the growing row of log books on the bookshelf record miles covered, new gear tested, and titbits of pilotage information which are always worth keeping for reference. One or two halcyon days in the sailing season live in the memory for years afterwards. But the details of the less perfect days just as worth preserving, too often get forgotten, unless the log is faithfully written up at the time. Noting the time of a passage from one landmark to another may seem irksome when under way, but such details are invaluable as a speed yardstick when planning other cruises.

The best deck log for a dinghy is a rectangular area of flat white painted on to a thwart on which information can be scribbled in pencil. Another use for this is to note, in advance the time of tides, and the direction and speed of streams along the course. At the end of the sail, the log entries can be transferred to a notebook and the day's scrawl erased.

The Reward

In a few years' time comes the reward for this work. In those brief phrases, disjointed and terse they may be, is some magic which brings it all back to the mind's eye. You can see again the colour of the land, and the shape of the sky, and remember how the spray flashed over the weather bow, how she swooped over a lively sea. An equal pleasure is the dropping of the anchor and the stowage of sails after a long passage, which never fail to bring the contentment of finality.

Appendix

Dinghy Cruising Association boat safety recommendations for cruising dinghies:

1. The boat should carry sufficient crew. One stone for each foot of waterline length is suggested as the minimum.

2. The boat should be stable enough to allow the whole crew to sit on the gunwale without dipping it under or the craft capsizing. As a guide, it is recommended that the beam should be not less than the cube root of the load waterline squared.

3. The boat should carry sufficient positive buoyancy to support itself together with stores and partially immersed crew, plus a reserve of not less than 112 lbs. This buoyancy should be so disposed that it is possible for the crew to put the boat back into sailing condition after capsizing or swamping.

4. A foredeck should be considered the minimum amount of permanent decking.

5. Mast, rigging, fittings, etc. must be strong enough to withstand capsizing forces.

6. The following equipment should be carried aboard:
   (a) Lifejackets for each member of the crew and one spare if possible.
   (b) Oilskins and plenty of warm clothes for each crew member.
   (c) An anchor (if a fisherman, one lb. for each foot of overall length is a good guide) and a strong warp (not less than 15 fathoms).
   (d) Two bailers, attached to the vessel by lanyards, or one bilge pump of substantial capacity and one bailer.
   (e) Two oars and rowlocks (secured to the vessel by lanyards) and one spare rowlock. PADDLES ARE NOT CONSIDERED A SATISFACTORY SUBSTITUTE.
   (f) Drinking water more than sufficient for the whole cruise. At least three pints per person per day.

7. The following equipment, additional to the items above, are advised for extended cruises:
   (a) Navigational equipment, such as charts, pilot books and the means of plotting a course.

   (b) A reliable steering compass and a pocket compass. If
      practicable the steering compass should be kept in one
      position and checked for deviation.
   (c) A barometer.
   (d) First Aid box and instructions.
   (e) Watertight containers holding daylight and night type flares,
      or other similarly effective distress signals.
   (f) A powerful light, to conform to international regulations
      and at least one spare torch.
   (g) A loud horn, bell, whistle, or other means of giving audible
      warning in thick weather.

8. Mainsail cloth should be at least one grade heavier than that
used on a similar sized racing dinghy and it must be practicable to
reef it at sea.

Index